Hiking
Carlsbad Caverns and Guadalupe Mountains
National Parks

*Published in partnership with
Trails Illustrated Maps and the Carlsbad
Caverns-Guadalupe Mountains Association.*

by
Bill Schneider

FALCON™

Falcon Press® Publishing Co., Inc.
Helena, Montana

A **FALCON** GUIDE

Falcon Press is continually expanding its list of recreational guidebooks. All books include detailed descriptions, accurate maps, and all the information necessary for enjoyable trips. You can order extra copies of this book and get information and prices for other Falcon guidebooks by writing Falcon Press, P.O. Box 1718, Helena, MT 59624 or calling toll free 1-800-582-2665. Also, please ask for a free copy of our current catalog.

All black-and-white photos by author unless stated otherwise.
Cover photos by Laurence Parent.
Front cover: Guadalupe Mountains National Park.
Back cover: Carlsbad Caverns National Park.

ISBN 1-56044-401-0

CAUTION

Outdoor recreation activities are by their very nature potentially hazardous. All participants in such activities must assume the responsibility for their own actions and safety. The information contained in this guidebook cannot replace sound judgment and good decision-making skills, which help reduce the risk exposure, nor does the scope of this book allow for disclosure of all the potential hazards and risks involved in such activities.

Learn as much as possible about the outdoor recreation activities you participate in, prepare for the unexpected, and be safe and cautious. The reward will be a safer and more enjoyable experience.

 Text pages printed on recycled paper.

"It seems that the strangeness and wonder are emphasized here in the desert . . . . The extreme clarity of the desert light is equaled by the extreme individualism of desert life forms."

—Edward Abbey

Books by Author

Where the Grizzly Walks
The Dakota Image
Hiking Montana
The Yellowstone River
The Tree Giants
The Flight of the Nez Perce
Hiking The Beartooths

CONTENTS

FOREWORD

More than 20 years ago I heard of an old timer in West Texas say that if you lived west of the Pecos River more than six months you would never want to live anywhere else. Such has been the case with me as I have lived and worked in three of our great national parks from the Mexican border country of the Big Bend to the high mountain peaks and mysterious caverns of the Guadalupe Mountains of West Texas and southern New Mexico.

The caverns and desert mountains of Carlsbad Caverns National Park and the high country of Guadalupe Mountains National Park lie within the northern-most region of what biologists call the Chihuahuan Desert. Here one can experience an enchanting part of North America offering an infinite variety of life forms and landscapes from the 8,749-foot summit of Guadalupe Peak, the highest peak in Texas, to more than 754 feet below the surface in the world-famous Big Room of Carlsbad Cavern.

This guidebook is a cooperative effort among the Carlsbad Caverns-Guadalupe Mountains Association, the National Park Service, and Falcon Press. Here you will find a nice summary of the numerous hiking and walking opportunities available to anyone with the desire to get close to the land carefully protected for the enjoyment, education, and inspiration of this and future generations.

Two walks that I would enthusiastically recommend are the paved trail through the Big Room of Carlsbad Cavern and the trail into McKittrick Canyon in the Guadalupe Mountains. Both offer scenery considered by many to be the best of New Mexico and Texas. When you go to these places, take your time and look closely. There are many wonders to be discovered by anyone with a little curiosity—and without a whole lot of effort.

No matter where you decide to hike or walk in these two great national parks, most importantly be sure to take in as much of this Chihuahuan Desert country as you can, for it is in the outdoors and along the trail that one experiences some of life's greatest moments. Here you can sit back and reflect on how you fit into the greater scheme of things and be inspired to do your part in helping to protect our natural world for future generations.

Let your life be enriched by the unique experience of the Guadalupe Mountains. Come back often and enjoy our great national parks.

—Rick Louis LoBello, Executive Director
Carlsbad Caverns-Guadalupe Mountains Association

ACKNOWLEDGMENTS

Any book—especially a trail guide—is a cooperative effort, and this book is no exception. I received invaluable help from many people.

First, I must thank Rick LoBello, executive director of the Carlsbad Caverns-Guadalupe Mountains Association (who made the book possible in the first place) and his associate Patsy Solwell.

Also, many thanks to Rich McCamant, Gary Veguist, Ed Greene, Dale Pate, Doug Ballou, Cookie Ballou, Rick Jackson, Dan Cantu, Vivian Sartori, Sam Franco, Dave Roemer, Rick Moraine, Karen Carswell, Linda Burlingame, and many others from the National Park Service who helped me during the research and review of the manuscript to assure accuracy.

And of course, I owe a big thank you to my staff at Falcon who endured my distraction with the book and helped me in a thousand ways to make it happen—especially Randall Green, our guidebook editor, Nick Baker, who edited the manuscript, and graphic artist Tony Moore, who did the maps and charts.

OVERVIEW MAP

An aerial view of the Guadalupe Mountains and the mouth of McKittrick Canyon.

Lechuguilla, common in both parks. NPS photo by D. Allen.

INTRODUCTION

The Great Reef

Driving along "the National Parks Highway" (U.S. Highway 62/180) through Guadalupe Pass between the Delaware and Guadalupe Mountains, through the eastern flank of Guadalupe Mountains National Park, and by the front door of Carlsbad Caverns National Park, you might glance off to the western horizon and see some hills but not realize that you have seen The Great Reef.

This is the home of two national parks, and it is one of the most cave-rich areas on the planet. It has so many caves that a cross-section would look like a 20-mile-long chunk of Swiss cheese.

It certainly looks like a mountain range, but technically, geologists call these 8,000-foot peaks the Capitan Reef. Geologists come from all over the world to see this giant, exposed formation composed of ancient fossils and riddled with caves.

The reef rises slowly in southeastern New Mexico, site of Carlsbad Caverns National Park, and extends southward into northwestern Texas where it abruptly ends with the venerable El Capitan at the southern edge of Guadalupe Mountains National Park. It seems the entire reef should be one national park, but 10 miles of the Lincoln National Forest separate the two parks.

The area doesn't have a Grand Teton or Denali, but so what? It has a special beauty that those famous mountains could never match. That beauty is embodied in the rugged individualism of desert flora and fauna and in the incredible diversity found in the parks, with the caves adding an extra treat to the mix.

When you go to Yellowstone, you study geysers. When you go to Point Reyes you learn about elephant seals. When you go to Olympic, you learn about rainforests. When you go to Hawaii Volcanoes, you learn about volcanoes. When you go to Carlsbad Caverns you learn about caves. And when you go to Guadalupe Mountains, you learn about the incredible diversity of desert flora and fauna found in this corner of the Chihuahuan Desert.

If that's not reason enough to come to Carlsbad Caverns or Guadalupe Mountains national parks, here's another small bonus: Neither park has entrance fees. However, there are camping fees for the drive-in campgrounds and a user fees for entering Carlsbad Caverns and other caves.

USING THIS GUIDEBOOK

This guidebook won't answer every question you have about your planned excursions to Carlsbad Caverns and Guadalupe Mountains national parks. But then, you probably do not want to know everything before you go, lest you eliminate the thrill of making your own discoveries. This book does, however, provide much of the basic information you need to plan you hiking trip.

TYPE OF TRIPS

Loop: Starts and finishes at the same trailhead, with no (or very little) retracing of your steps.

Shuttle: A point-to-point trip that requires two vehicles or an arrangement to be picked up at the end of the trail at a designated time. One way to manage the logistical problems of shuttles is to arrange for another party to start at the other end of the trail, meet at a pre-determined point on the trail and trade keys, and when finished hiking, drive each other's vehicle home.

Out-and-Back: Traveling to a specific destination and then retracing your steps back to the trailhead.

DISTANCES

In Guadalupe Mountains National Park, distances used in this book come from NPS handouts and Trails Illustrated maps. In Carlsbad Caverns National Park, distances come from NPS handouts and signs and, in a few cases, estimates made from topo maps. Keep in mind that distance is often less important than difficulty. A rocky, 2-mile uphill climb can take longer than 4 miles on a well-contoured trail on flat terrain.

RATINGS

The estimates of difficulty should serve as general guidelines only, not the final word. What is difficult to one person may be easy to the next. In this guidebook, difficulty ratings consider both how long and how strenuous the route is. Here are general definitions of the ratings.

Easy—Suitable for any hiker, including small children or the elderly, without serious elevation gain, hazardous sections, or places where the trail is faint.

Moderate—Suitable for hikers who have some experience and at least an average fitness level, probably not suitable for small children or the elderly unless they have above-average level of fitness, perhaps with some short sections where the trail is difficult to follow, and often with some hills to climb.

Difficult: Suitable for experienced hikers with above-average fitness level, often with sections of the trail that are difficult to follow or some off-trail sections that could

Cairns lead the way through the junipers dotting the plateau above Yucca Canyon.

require knowledge of route-finding with topo map and compass, sometimes with serious elevation gain, and possibly some hazardous conditions.

FOLLOWING FAINT TRAILS

Some trails in both parks receive infrequent use and can fade away in places. Don't panic. Usually, these sections are short, and you can look ahead to see where the trail goes. If so, focus on that landmark and don't worry about being off the trail for a short distance.

You should also watch for other indicators that you are indeed on the right route, even if the trail isn't clearly visible. In Carlsbad Caverns and Guadalupe Mountains, watch for cairns (strategically located piles of rocks), which are often used to mark faint trails.

SHARING

We all want our own wilderness area all to ourselves, but that only happens in our dreams. Lots of people use the national parks, and to give everybody an equal chance of having a great experience, we all must work at politely sharing the wilderness.

For example, hikers must share trails with backcountry horsemen. Both groups have every right to be on the trail. Keep in mind that horses and other stock animals are much less maneuverable than hikers, so it becomes the hiker's responsibility to yield the right-of-way. When you see horses ahead on the trail or when they catch you from behind, move uphill from the trail about 20 feet and quietly let the stock animals pass.

Another example of politely sharing the wilderness is courteously choosing your campsite. If you get to a popular camping area late in the day and all good camp-sites are taken, don't crowd in on another camper. This is most aggravating, as these

The 1989 El Capitan Fire caused by a lightning strike. Other fires in the parks have been caused by careless park visitors, so be very careful with fire. NPS photo by J. Bassinger.

sites rightfully go on a first-come, first-served basis. If you're late, you have the responsibility to move on or take a campsite a respectable distance away from other campers, even if it's a less desirable site. In Guadalupe Mountains National Park, designated backcountry campgrounds have as many as eight tent sites. Try to pick one as far away from other campers as possible.

SPECIAL RULES AND REGULATIONS FOR BACKCOUNTRY USE

Carlsbad Caverns and Guadalupe Mountains national parks have strict regulations to protect the fragile environment. Please follow these rules carefully.

- Pets, with or without a leash, are prohibited on all backcountry trails.

- Do not drive vehicles off established roads.

- The collecting, destroying, or defacing of any mineral, plant, animal, or historic or archaeological artifact is prohibited.

- All firearms, or any implement designed to discharge missiles, are prohibited.

- Entry into any cave in the backcountry without written permission from the park superintendent is prohibited.

- Campfires are prohibited.

- All backcountry campers must have a free backcountry camping permit. In Guadalupe Mountains, backpackers must use designated campsites. In Carlsbad

Caverns, you must camp at least 0.25 mile from and out of sight of any road. You can get backcountry camping permits at any park visitor center or ranger station. Hikers can only get permits in person, no more than 24 hours in advance.

• At Carlsbad Caverns, hikers must camp at least 100 yards from any natural water source due to wildlife drinking habits. At Guadalupe Mountains, campers must use designated sites.

• If possible, return your backcountry permit at any park ranger station or visitor center when you leave the backcountry so rangers will know you have returned safely.

FINDING MAPS

Good maps are easy to find, and they are essential to any wilderness trip. For safety reasons, you need maps for route-finding and for "staying found." For non-safety reasons, you would not want to miss out on the unending joy of mindlessly whittling away untold hours staring at a topo map and wondering what it's like here and there.

For trips into the Carlsbad Caverns and Guadalupe Mountains national parks, you have two good choices for maps—U.S. Geological Survey (USGS) topo maps and Trails Illustrated maps. The well-prepared wilderness travelers will take both. Guadalupe Mountains National Park also has a free map that is adequate for many hikes.

You can find maps at the following locations:

TRAILS ILLUSTRATED MAPS: To obtain Trails Illustrated maps, call toll free 1-800-962-1643.

USGS: Available at sporting goods stores in the local area or write directly to the USGS at the following address:

> Map Distribution
> U.S. Geological Survey
> Box 25286, Federal Center
> Denver, CO 80225

FOR MORE INFORMATION

The best source of more information is the National Park Service. Use the following addresses and phone numbers.

> Carlsbad Caverns National Park   Phone: 505-785-2232
> 3225 National Park Highway
> Carlsbad, NM 88220

> Guadalupe Mountains National Park   Phone: 915-828-3251
> H.C. 60, Box 400
> Salt Flat, TX 79847-9400

VACATION PLANNER

CARLSBAD CAVERNS NATIONAL PARK

TRAILS FOR PEOPLE WITH MOBILITY IMPAIRMENTS:
Chihuahuan Desert
Nature Trail

EASY DAY HIKES:
Guano Road Trail
Juniper Ridge

MODERATE DAY TRIPS:
Rattlesnake Canyon

DIFFICULT DAY TRIPS:
Yucca Canyon
Slaughter Canyon
Guadalupe Ridge

OVERNIGHT TRIPS:
Yucca Canyon
Slaughter Canyon
Guadalupe Ridge
Rattlesnake Canyon

New Mexico century plant only blooms once, usually after 20 or 30 years, not 100 years as rumored. NPS photo by D Allen.

GUADALUPE MOUNTAINS NATIONAL PARK

TRAILS FOR PEOPLE WITH MOBILITY IMPAIRMENTS:

Smith Spring (to Mazanita
Spring only)
The Pinery

EASY DAY TRIPS:

McKittrick Canyon Nature
Trail
Indian Meadows Nature Trail
McKittrick Canyon (to Pratt
Lodge)
Smith Spring

MODERATE DAY TRIPS:

Devil's Hall
Salt Basin Overlook
Foothills
Lost Peak
McKittrick Canyon (to The
Grotto)

DIFFICULT DAY TRIPS:

Guadalupe Peak
El Capitan
Hunter Peak
The Bowl
McKittrick Canyon (to The
Notch)
Permian Reef
The Tejas Trail

OVERNIGHT TRIPS:

Pine Springs to McKittrick
Canyon
Guadalupe Peak
Bush Mountain
Hunter Peak
The Bowl
McKittrick Ridge
Permian Reef
The Tejas Trail
Blue Ridge
The Marcus Trail
Dog Canyon to McKittrick
Canyon

AUTHOR'S RECOMMENDATIONS

CARLSBAD CAVERNS NATIONAL PARK

FOR PARENTS WHO WANT A REALLY EASY DAY HIKE:

    Chihuahua Desert Nature Trail

FOR PEOPLE WHO WANT AN EASY—BUT NOT TOO EASY— DAY HIKE:

    Juniper Ridge
    Guano Road Trail

FOR PEOPLE WHO CAN'T DECIDE BETWEEN A LONG HIKE OR A SHORT HIKE, SO OBVIOUSLY NEED A MODERATELY DIFFICULT HIKE:

    Rattlesnake Canyon

FOR PEOPLE WHO WANT A LONG, HARD DAY HIKE SO AT THE END OF THE DAY THEY CAN EAT ANYTHING THEY WANT FOR DINNER AND NOT FEEL GUILTY:

    Yucca Canyon
    Slaughter Canyon
    Guadalupe Ridge

FOR THAT FIRST NIGHT IN THE WILDERNESS:

    Rattlesnake Canyon

FOR PHOTOGRAPHERS:

    Rattlesnake Canyon
    Guadalupe Ridge
    Yucca Canyon

FOR PEOPLE WHO WANT A MULTI-DAY BACKCOUNTRY ADVENTURE:

    Guadalupe Ridge
    Slaughter Canyon (loop route)

FOR TRAIL RUNNERS AND POWER HIKERS:

    Guano Road Trail
    Guadalupe Ridge

GUADALUPE MOUNTAINS NATIONAL PARK

FOR PARENTS WHO WANT A REALLY EASY DAY HIKE:

The Pinery
McKittrick Canyon Nature Trail
Indian Meadows Nature Trail

FOR PEOPLE WHO WANT AN EASY—BUT NOT TOO EASY—DAY HIKE:

Smith Spring
McKittrick Canyon (to Pratt Lodge)

FOR PEOPLE WHO CAN'T DECIDE BETWEEN A LONG HIKE OR A SHORT HIKE, SO OBVIOUSLY NEED A MODERATELY DIFFICULT HIKE:

Devil's Hall
Salt Basin Overlook
Foothills
Lost Peak

FOR PEOPLE WHO WHAT A LONG, HARD DAY HIKE SO AT THE END OF THE DAY THEY CAN EAT ANYTHING THEY WANT FOR DINNER AND NOT FEEL GUILTY:

Guadalupe Peak
McKittrick Canyon (to The Notch)
Salt Basin Overlook
Hunter Peak
The Tejas Trail
El Capitan (one way)
Permian Reef

FOR THAT FIRST NIGHT IN THE WILDERNESS:

Hunter Peak
The Tejas Trail

FOR PHOTOGRAPHERS:

Guadalupe Peak
McKittrick Canyon (to The Notch)
El Capitan
Salt Basin Overlook
Hunter Peak
Permian Reef

FOR PEOPLE WHO WANT A MULTI-DAY BACKCOUNTRY ADVENTURE:

El Capitan (out & back)
Pine Springs to McKittrick Canyon
Bush Mountain
Dog Canyon to McKittrick Canyon
The Tejas Trail

FOR PEOPLE WHO WANT TO SEE THE WILDEST PART OF THE GUADALUPE MOUNTAINS:

Bush Mountain
The Marcus Trail
Blue Ridge

FOR TRAIL RUNNERS AND POWER HIKERS:

Salt Basin Overlook
Pine Springs to McKittrick
  Canyon
Guadalupe Peak
McKittrick Canyon (to The
  Grotto)
El Capitan
Dog Canyon to McKittrick
  Canyon
The Tejas Trail
Permian Reef

FOR PEOPLE WHO WANT TO WALK ALL THE WAY THROUGH THE GUADALUPE MOUNTAINS:

The Tejas Trail
Pine Springs to McKittrick
  Canyon

LEAVE NO TRACE

Going into the desert is like visiting a famous museum. You obviously do not want to leave your mark on an art treasure in the museum. If everybody going through the museum left one little mark, the piece of art would be quickly destroyed. And of what value is a big building full of trashed art? The same goes for a pristine wilderness, such as the Chihuahuan Desert of Carlsbad Caverns and Guadalupe Mountains national parks, which is as magnificent as any masterpiece of any artist. If we all left just one little mark, the wilderness would soon be despoiled.

A wilderness can accommodate lots of human use as long as everybody behaves. But a few thoughtless or uninformed visitors can ruin it for the rest of us. An important addition to the hiker's checklist is proper wilderness manners. Don't leave home without them.

All wilderness users have a responsibility to know and follow the rules of No Trace Camping. An important source of these guidelines, including the most recent research, can be found in the book, *Wild Country Companion*. (Ordering information in the back of this book.)

Nowadays, most wilderness users want to walk softly, but some aren't aware that they have poor manners. Often, their actions are dictated by the outdated understanding of a past generation of campers who cut green boughs for evening shelters, built campfires with fire rings, and dug trenches around tents. In the 1950s, these "camping

In backcountry campsites in Guadalupe Mountains, the NPS has designated and flattened out tentsites such as this one at the Blue Ridge Camp.

rules" may have been acceptable, but they leave long-lasting scars. Today, such behavior is absolutely unacceptable. The wilderness is shrinking, and the number of users is mushrooming. More and more camping areas show the unsightly signs of this trend.

Thus, a new code of ethics is growing out of necessity to cope with the unending waves of people wanting a perfect wilderness experience. Today, we all must leave no signs that we have gone before. Canoeists can look behind them and see no trace of their passing. Hikers should have the same goal. Enjoy the wildness, but leave no trace of your visit.

Most of us know better than to litter—in or out of the wilderness. Be sure you leave nothing, regardless of how small it is, along the trail or at the campsite. This means you should pack out everything, including orange peels, flip tops, cigarette butts, and gum wrappers. Also, pick up any trash that others leave behind.

Follow the main trail. Avoid cutting switchbacks and walking on vegetation beside the trail. In the desert, some of the terrain is very fragile, so stay on the trail. And don't pick up "souvenirs," such as rocks, antlers, or wildflowers. The next person wants to see them, too. Besides, this violates park regulations.

This goes triple for any archeological sites. These are very precious and extra fragile. Don't even go near them, and obviously, do not disturb the aging signs of early cultures. Park regulations strictly prohibit disturbing archeological sites.

Avoid making loud noises that may disturb others. Remember, sound travels easily to the other side of the canyon. Be courteous.

Be careful with food wastes to prevent unsightly messes and bad odors.

If you use toilet paper, you need to pack it out with the rest of your garbage. In many hiking areas, you can safely use white, unscented paper and bury it 6-8 inches along with human waste, but at Carlsbad Caverns and Guadalupe Mountains, the topsoil is so thin, that you really only have one option—packing it out. Bring along zip-lock bags for this purpose.

Finally, and perhaps most important, strictly follow the pack-in pack-out rule. If you carry something into the backcountry, consume it or carry it out.

Leave no trace—and then, put your ear to the ground in the wilderness and listen carefully. Thousands of people who will follow you are thanking you for your courtesy and good sense.

BE PREPARED

The Scouts have been guided for decades by, perhaps, the best single piece of safety advice—Be Prepared! For starters, this means carrying survival and first-aid materials, proper clothing, compass, and topographic map—and knowing how to use them.

Perhaps the second-best advice is to tell somebody where you're going and when you plan to return. Pilots must file flight plans before every trip, and anybody venturing into a blank spot on the map should do the same. File your "flight plan" with a friend or relative before taking off.

Close behind your flight plan and being prepared with proper equipment is physical conditioning. Being fit not only makes wilderness travel more fun, it makes it safer.

To whet your appetite for more knowledge of wilderness safety and preparedness, here are a few basic tips.

• Check the weather forecast. Be careful not to get caught at high altitude by a bad storm, and watch the cloud formations closely, so you don't get stranded on a ridgeline during a lightning storm. Avoid traveling during prolonged periods of cold weather.

• Avoid traveling alone in the wilderness.

• Keep your party together.

• Know the preventive measures, symptoms, and treatment of hypothermia, the silent killer.

• Study basic survival and first-aid before leaving home.

• Don't eat wild plants unless you are positive of their identification.

• Before you leave find out as much as you can about the route, especially the potential hazards.

• Don't exhaust yourself or other members of your party by traveling too far or too fast. Let the slowest person set the pace.

• Don't wait until you're confused to look at your maps. Follow them as you go along, from the moment you start moving up the trail, so you have a continual fix on your location.

• If you get lost, don't panic. Sit down and relax for a few minutes while you carefully check your topo map and take a reading with your compass. Confidently plan your next move. It's often smart to retrace your steps until you find familiar ground, even if you think it might make the trip longer. Lots of people get temporarily lost in the wilderness and survive—usually by calmly and rationally dealing with the situation.

• Stay clear of all wild animals.

Last but not least, don't forget that the best defense against unexpected hazards is knowledge. Read up on the latest in wilderness safety information, in the recently published book, *Wild Country Companion*. Check the back of this guidebook for ordering information.

LIGHTNING

Do not be caught on a ridge or a mountain top, under large solitary trees, in the open, or near open water during a lightning storm. Try to seek shelter in a low-lying area, ideally in a dense stand of small, uniformly sized trees. Stay away from anything that might attract lightning, such as metal tent poles, graphite fishing rods, or pack frames.

SURVIVAL KIT

A survival kit should include: compass, whistle, matches in a waterproof container, cigarette lighter, candle, signal mirror, fire starter, aluminum foil, water purification tablets, space blanket, and flare.

FIRST-AID KIT

Your first-aid kit should include: sewing needle, a snake-bite kit, aspirin, antibacterial ointment, two antiseptic swabs, two butterfly bandages, adhesive tape, four adhesive strips, four gauze pads, two triangular bandages, asprin, codeine tablets, two inflatable splints, moleskin, one roll three-inch gauze, CPR shield, rubber gloves, and lightweight first-aid instructions.

THE SILENT KILLER

Be aware of the danger of hypothermia—a condition in which the body's internal temperature drops below normal. It can lead to mental and physical collapse and death.

Hypothermia is caused by exposure to cold and is aggravated by wetness, wind, and exhaustion. The moment you begin to lose heat faster than your body produces it, you're suffering from exposure. Your body starts involuntary exercise such as shivering to stay warm, and your body makes involuntary adjustments to preserve normal temperature in vital organs, restricting blood flow in the extremities. Both responses drain your energy reserves. The only way to stop the drain is to reduce the degree of exposure.

With full-blown hypothermia, your energy reserves are exhausted, cold reaches the brain, depriving you of good judgment and reasoning power. You won't be aware that this is happening. You lose control of your hands. Your internal temperature slides downward. Without treatment, this slide leads to stupor, collapse, and death.

To defend against hypothermia, stay dry. When clothes get wet, they lose about 90 percent of their insulating value. Wool loses relatively less heat; cotton, down, and some synthetics lose more. Choose rain clothes that cover the head, neck, body, and legs, and provide good protection against wind-driven rain. Most hypothermia cases develop in air temperatures between 30 and 50 degrees Fahrenheit, but hypothermia can develop in warmer temperatures.

If your party is exposed to wind, cold, and wet, think hypothermia. Watch yourself and others for these symptoms: Uncontrollable fits of shivering; vague, slow, slurred speech; memory lapses; incoherence; immobile, fumbling hands; frequent stumbling or a lurching gait; drowsiness (to sleep is to die); apparent exhaustion; and inability to get up after a rest.

When a member of your party has hypothermia, he/she may deny any problem. Believe the symptoms, not the victim. Even mild symptoms demand treatment, as follows:

- Get the victim out of the wind and rain.

- Strip off all wet clothes.

- If the victim is only mildly impaired, give him or her warm drinks. Then, get him/her in warm clothes and a warm sleeping bag. Place well-wrapped water bottles filled with heated water close to the victim.

- If the victim is badly impaired, attempt to keep him/her awake. Put the victim in a sleeping bag with another person—both naked. If you have a double bag, put two warm people in with the victim.

DESERT HIKING

Carlsbad Caverns and Guadalupe Mountains national parks are part of the Chihuahuan Desert. The high country of the Guadalupes is technically in another biome, but there is still desert hiking getting there and back, so prepare for the desert environment. That means having the right equipment and clothing, but it also means being mentally prepared.

For starters, you should make one major mental adjustment. The only water you will ever drink in the desert is the water you carry with you. That differs significantly with most hiking areas where you can bank on getting water from a stream or lake and purifying or filtering it to make it safe to drink.

This is actually a difficult attitude adjustment for many people accustomed to hiking in non-desert climates, especially on their first trip to the desert. It won't be long, however, before the special character of the desert creeps into your body and takes root, and then, you love the place, no matter how hot and dry it is.

Most hiking in northern climates occurs during the summer months, particularly July and August. This might be the worst time to go to the desert. The best time is either the spring (March, April or May), when the fabulous desert wildflowers bloom or in the fall (September, October or November), when the fall foliage is out in full, color. Also, the spring and fall temperatures usually drop to a level to make hiking much more enjoyable than summer months.

Watch out for the Western diamondback rattlesnake, found in both parks. The rattlesnake is a key part of the natural system. NPS photo by B. Wauer.

Hiking in the desert is, simply put, more exercise. It's also more limited by the hiker's physical strength and stamina than hiking in moist climates. You really can't go lightweight because you need to carry your water.

Experts recommend taking one gallon of water per person per day. For many people, this essentially limits the length of your trip to two or three nights. A gallon of water weighs about eight pounds, so on a three-day trip (two nights out), for example, each hiker would have to carry at least twenty pounds of water.

If you're planning a longer trip and the weight of your pack is stretching your physical abilities, cut out weight in other ways instead of reducing water supply. For example, abandon optional equipment like extra camera gear or binoculars—or at least take lightweight models. Take fewer clothes—it won't kill you to wear the same shirt two days in a row. Shop for a super-lightweight tent and sleeping bag. Go with the lighter but perhaps less comfortable sleeping pad.

It might be tempting to leave your tent home to save weight, but a tent can be a life-saver if bad weather blows in. However, you can take a lightweight, three-season tent to save weight, or you can substitute a lightweight four-person tent instead of taking two smaller tents that together weigh more.

Food presents a special challenge. The lightest food of all (freeze-dried meals or dehydrated foods like pasta, rice, and oatmeal) all take water to prepare. This means you have to add to your water supply or use alternative foods that don't require extra water.

This might seem like heresy to backpacking gourmands, but one alternative is to take the no-cooking option. Prepare evening meals in leakproof containers or make sandwiches. Plan on snacking for breakfast and lunch. This essentially means snacking all the time instead of cooking. This might seem radical, but you can save weight in two ways—less water and less gas for your stove. You could, actually, leave your stove and gas home completely if you're sure of the weather forecast and have no chance of running into cold weather.

Although the lack of water presents the biggest challenge for the hiker, the abundance of sunshine also requires special preparation and planning. Two pieces of equipment that might be optional elsewhere, sunglasses and sunscreen, are essential for desert hiking.

Don't underestimate the power of the desert sun. You might think you have a tan and don't need sunscreen, but you're probably wrong. You'll be unpleasantly shocked at how fast you can burn, and a bad sunburn, besides being unhealthy for other reasons, will certainly take the fun out of the rest of your vacation. To be safe, use sunscreen in the 25 to 50 range.

Also, pay attention to the type of clothing you wear. Go "light and white," and try for natural fibers like cotton whenever possible. Even though it's better to wear long pants and shirt to cut down the amount of skin exposed to the sun, many people prefer the comfort of shorts and short sleeves.

The sun isn't the only reason to wear long pants. If you're going cross-country or on a rough trail like the Blue Ridge Loop in the Guadalupes or the Slaughter Canyon in Carlsbad Caverns, you definitely should wear long pants. If you don't, sotol, catclaw, cholla, and other desert flora (most species armed with spines) will be constantly taking little nicks out of your legs. Your wounds will eventually heal, but wearing long pants will be less painful. For example, lechuguilla, a knife-sharp agave, can penetrate the skin and leave a spine that can be very difficult to remove.

Although both parks have rattlesnakes, most hikers rarely see one. During the day in the summer and in winter, they usually hide away under rocks and in cracks and crevices. You're most likely to find a rattlesnake on summer evenings. Most rattlesnakes are not aggressive and will not strike unless stepped on or provoked. If you don't hike at night or don't stick hands or feet in crevices and under ledges, you probably won't get bit. If you do see a rattlesnake, stay clear and don't harm it.

Another piece of equipment essential for enjoying the desert is good footwear. You don't need the extra-heavy boots mountain climbers wear, but you need sturdy boots with at least ankle height. Running or cross-training shoes might suffice for easier trips, but anything long and rough calls for sturdier boots, even more so than forested hiking areas in northern mountain ranges.

To enjoy desert hiking even more, take advantage of the early morning or late evening. The desert light is the purest early and late in the day, and usually the temperature drops to a more tolerable level. Plus, you stand a better chance of seeing desert wildlife. Most desert fauna is nocturnal, and even diurnal species usually remain inactive during the mid-day.

Turkey vultures, common in both parks. NPS photo.

HIKER'S CHECKLIST

Hiking Equipment: Equipment does not have to be new or fancy (or expensive), but make sure you test everything before you leave home.

Equipment Checklist for Day Hiking in the Desert:
- ☐ Day pack or fanny pack
- ☐ Water bottles
- ☐ Compass
- ☐ Maps
- ☐ Toilet trowel
- ☐ Toilet paper
- ☐ Sun block and lip lotion
- ☐ Binoculars*
- ☐ Camera and extra film*
- ☐ Flashlight and extra batteries
- ☐ Pocket knife and tweezers
- ☐ Sunglasses
- ☐ Survival kit
- ☐ First-aid kit

Added Equipment for Overnight Trips in the Desert:
- ☐ Tent and waterproof fly
- ☐ Sleeping bag (20 degrees or warmer) and stuff sack
- ☐ Sleeping pad
- ☐ Cooking pots and pot holder
- ☐ Extra water bottles
- ☐ Full-size backpack
- ☐ Cup, bowl, and eating utensils
- ☐ Lightweight camp stove and adequate fuel
- ☐ Garbage sacks
- ☐ Zip-lock bags
- ☐ Paper towels*
- ☐ Nylon cord (50 ft.)
- ☐ Small towel
- ☐ Personal toilet kit
- ☐ Notebook and pencil*

Special Equipment for Cave Routes:
- ☐ Powerful flashlight
- ☐ Back-up flashlight
- ☐ Two sets of extra batteries
- ☐ Sweatshirt or light coat
- ☐ Shoes with good grips

(* = optional).

☐ Knee pads and elbow pads
☐ Long sleeve shirt
☐ Long pants

Clothing: In general, strive for natural fibers such as cotton and wool with earth-toned instead of bright colors. Dig around in the closet for something dull. Your wilderness partners will appreciate it. Try out the clothing before leaving home to make sure everything fits loosely with no chafing. In particular, make sure your boots are broken in, lest they break you on the first day of the hike.

Clothing for Day Hiking in the Desert:
☐ Large-brimmed hat or cap
☐ Sturdy hiking boots
☐ Light, natural fiber socks
☐ Lightweight, light-colored hiking shorts or long pants
☐ Light colored, long-sleeve shirt
☐ Lightweight, windproof coat
☐ Raingear
☐ Mittens or gloves*

Added Clothing for Overnight Trips in the Desert:
☐ Warm hat (i.e. stocking cap)
☐ Long underwear
☐ Water-resistant, windproof wilderness coat
☐ Sweater and/or insulated vest
☐ Long pants
☐ One pair of socks for each day, plus one extra pair
☐ Underwear
☐ Extra shirts
☐ Sandals or lightweight shoes for wearing in camp

Food: For day hiking, bring high-energy snacks such as raisins or granola bars for lunching along the way. For overnight trips, bring enough food, including high-energy snacks for lunching during the day, but don't overburden yourself with too much food. Plan meals carefully, bringing just enough food, plus some emergency rations. Freeze-dried foods are the lightest and safest, but they're expensive, require extra water, and aren't really necessary. Don't forget hot and cold drinks. Try to minimize food that requires extra water to prepare.

Water: With no available water sources in either Carlsbad Caverns or Guadalupe Mountains national parks, water becomes the most critical piece of equipment on your checklist. To be safe, take one gallon per person per day (24 hours). Don't drink too much of your water early in your trip, but at the same time, drink adequately and steadily throughout the day to avoid dehydration.

(* = optional).

HORSES

Horses are allowed on backcountry trails in both Carlsbad Caverns and Guadalupe Mountains under special regulations. About 60 percent of the trails in Guadalupe Mountains and most of the trails in Carlsbad Caverns are open to horses, but an essential part of planning a trip involving horses or other stock animals should be a call to the park headquarters for specific regulations.

Some trails are simply too hazardous, and these have been closed to horse use. In other areas, trails pass through a particularly fragile environment intolerant to horse use. For example, horse manure may introduce exotic plant species that can displace native vegetation.

Guadalupe Mountains has prepared a special "Horseback Riding" brochure explaining in detail the park regulations. It also includes an excellent trail map showing which trails are open to horses and ranking the trails for difficulty.

Although you should definitely call for specific information, here is a brief checklist of special needs and regulations for horse use in Carlsbad Caverns and Guadalupe Mountains national parks.

• All rides in the parks require thorough preparation. Improper equipment, poor conditioning, or disregard for weather conditions can result in an unpleasant or dangerous experience.

• Both parks require a free backcountry use permit for all horse use of backcountry trails. You can get the permits at any park visitor center or ranger station.

• Horse use is restricted to day use only. No horses can be kept in the backountry overnight.

• Both parks have stock corrals, but you must call ahead for reservations. Manure dropped in the corrals must be cleaned up and deposited in a marked receptacle before leaving the park. Trail riders must use the trailheads at these corrals instead of transporting horses to other trailheads.

• No feed is available in either park.

• Water is available at corrals, but no water is available along backcountry trails in either park.

• All stock should be properly shod before arriving at the park. Bring shoeing tools and supplies. Almost all trails have rocky sections.

• Groups are limited to 10 animals or less. This is to reduce potential conflicts between trail riders and hikers and to reduce trail damage.

• All stock must remain on designated trails.

- All livestock must meet state vaccination requirements, and copies of vaccination documents must be in your possession. Nursing colts may not accompany their mothers on park trails, and loose herding is not permitted.

- Special use permits are required for commercial groups.

- No horses are available for rent in the vicinity of either park.

CARLSBAD CAVERNS NATIONAL PARK

OVERVIEW MAP

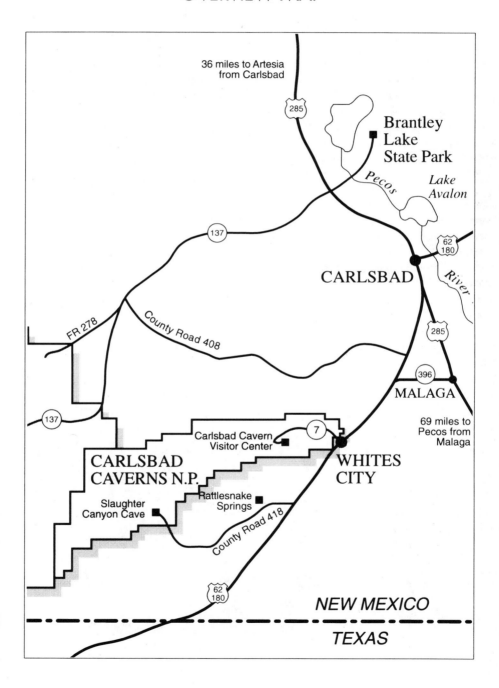

36 miles to Artesia
from Carlsbad

285

Brantley
Lake
State Park

Pecos

*Lake
Avalon*

137

62
180

CARLSBAD

River

FR 278

County Road 408

285

396

MALAGA

137

7

Carlsbad Cavern
Visitor Center

69 miles to
Pecos from
Malaga

CARLSBAD
CAVERNS N.P.

WHITES
CITY

Rattlesnake
Springs

Slaughter
Canyon Cave

County Road 418

62
180

NEW MEXICO

TEXAS

OVERVIEW

Carlsbad Caverns National Park lies in the northern reaches of The Capitan Reef, the world's largest exposed fossil reef, named for the prominent landmark El Capitan at the southern end. The park not only hosts the famous Carlsbad Caverns, but it has 81 other caves, most with no (or limited) public access. And on top of that—literally—the park has 46,755 surface acres with about 50 miles of backcountry trails.

Carlsbad Caverns is certainly one of the treasures of the National Park System. Obviously, many people agree because hordes come to see the cave each summer. And the National Park Service has offered up the wonders of Carlsbad Caverns on a silver platter. With elevators, beautifully contoured paths, detailed interpretive displays, and rangers anxious to answer all your questions, the NPS spreads out the story of Carlsbad Caverns for all to enjoy.

At Carlsbad Caverns, you can enjoy the depths of the cave in two distinctly different ways. You can go mainstream tourist route and take one of the self-guided tours or you can get down-and-dirty and take a guided tour of what is, in essence, "an underground trail" that leaves you with the sense of what it must have been like for that first person who entered the cave with a torch or kerosene lantern. It can also leave you as dirty as a mud wrestler, so wear old clothes.

After experiencing the cave, however, you still have not seen all that Carlsbad Caverns National Park has to offer. You shouldn't leave the park without hiking below *and* above the surface.

Besides the obvious contrast between surface and subsurface, there is another big difference. The subterranean routes are elbow-to-elbow in the busy summer season while up on the surface, the trails are deserted. You can hike all day in gorgeous desert environs and perhaps not see another hiker—certainly a rarity in America's ultra-popular National Park System.

This is the first guidebook to the trails of Carlsbad Caverns National Park, and it wasn't published until 1996. Once you get out there on these trails, you'll find that fact pretty incredible.

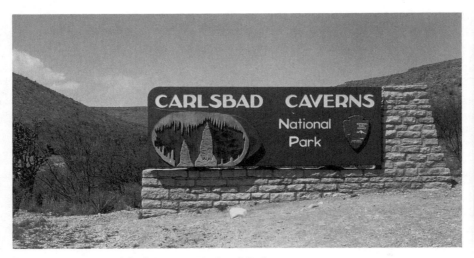

Entrance sign to Carlsbad Caverns National Park.

From El Paso, Texas, drive northeast 142 miles on U.S. Highway 62/180 to Whites City, New Mexico. At Whites City, turn west and go 7 miles on a paved park road which deadends at the park headquarters where you'll also find a visitor center, cafe, gift shop, bookstore, the Bat Flight Amphitheater, and the cave entrance. From Carlsbad, New Mexico, drive south 20 miles on U.S. Hwy. 62/180 to Whites City, then west to the park headquarters. If you're flying in and renting a car, it's best to use the El Paso airport. All services (gas station, grocery store, restaurants, motels, etc.) are available at Whites City.

SURFACE ROUTES

1 CHIHUAHUAN DESERT NATURE TRAIL

Type of trail:	Self-guided loop
Type of trip:	Day hike.
Total distance:	0.5 mile.
Difficulty:	Easy.
Elevation change:	Minimal.
Time required:	Half hour.
Maps:	Trails Illustrated Carlsbad Caverns Map, USGS Carlsbad Caverns.
Starting point:	The Bat Flight Amphitheater at park headquarters.

Chihuahuan Desert Nature Trail with Carlsbad Caverns Headquarters and the Bat Flight Amiphitheater in the background.

Finding the trailhead: Park in the visitor center parking lot. The trail starts either at the west end of the parking lot or at the Bat Flight Amphitheater.

The trail: This trail is for everybody. It's entirely paved, has lots of interesting interpretation, and is accessible to people with mobility impairments. You can take the short loop in either direction, but the interpretive signs are set up in a counterclockwise sequence. There are benches for relaxing along the way. In one stop, about halfway around, you get a expansive view of the desert basin to the southeast.

If you plan to watch the grand exit of bats from Carlsbad or if you plan to visit the cave, plan on getting to the headquarters area a half-hour early and take a leisurely stroll around this trail first. The trail is closed during the bat flight to avoid disturbing the bats.

The interpretive signs along the trail give you a great introduction into desert flora and how native cultures used desert plants. You can learn how early residents roasted sotol hearts, wove diapers from juniper bark and rope from lechuguilla leaves, made cough medicine from ocotillo and smashed soap from the roots of the torrey yucca. You can also see why they called the Torrey yucca the "Spanish Dagger" and, just as obviously, how the catclaw acacia earned its name.

About halfway around the half-mile trail, you can see a fenced-off area protecting a second natural entrance to the caverns. Just east of the fenced off area (not accessible by trail) lie two shafts blasted into the bat cave. Guano miners created these artificial entrances (now sealed) to more easily remove the guano, but it turned out to be self-defeating. The artificial entrances upset the delicate habitat used for centuries by the bats. The end result was, regrettably and ironically, a reduced bat population and, of course, less guano.

---

2 GUANO ROAD TRAIL

Type of trail:	Shuttle.
Type of trip:	Day hike.
Total distance:	3.5 miles.
Difficulty:	Easy.
Elevation change:	710 feet.
Time required:	2-3 hours.
Maps:	Trails Illustrated Carlsbad Caverns Map, USGS Carlsbad Caverns.
Starting point:	The Bat Flight Amphitheater at park headquarters or at the west end of the campground at Whites City.

Finding the trailhead: The trailhead at the park headquarters is easy to find. The trail starts right at the Bat Flight Amphitheater where the Chihuahuan Desert Nature Trail ends. In fact, the first 0.25 mile is also part of the Chihuahuan Desert Nature Trail. However, the trailhead at Whites City is not as easy to find. The trail starts at the westernmost part of a private campground on the west end of Whites City. Watch for a new sign at the Whites City trailhead. You can also easily see what looks like an old jeep road heading up the hill from the campground. That's the trail.

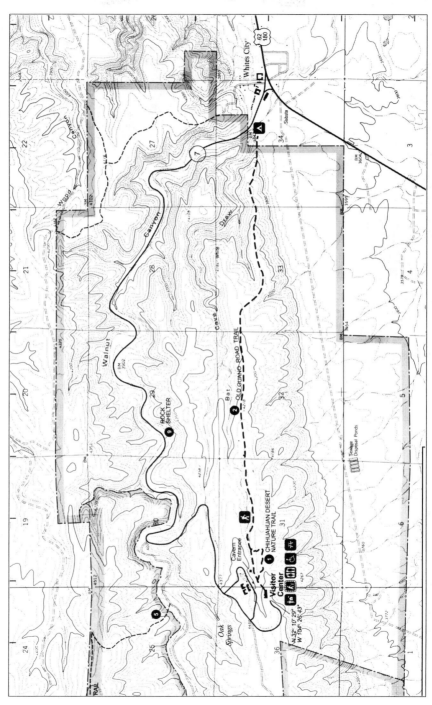

The beginning of the Guano Trail at the west end of Whites City.

The trail: This might be the most convenient way to experience the "other" Carlsbad Caverns, the world above ground. This trail follows the ridge just south of the paved road from Whites City to the park headquarters. Even though you never get far from the highway, much of the trail is out of sight and sound of the road. The trail does not appear on the Carlsbad Caverns USGS topo map.

You can start at either end, but for the easiest route, start at the Bat Flight Amphitheater. This makes the trail a gradual downhill walk the entire way.

Since this is a shuttle, transportation can be a problem. One idea is to take your trip into the caverns and then, instead of your entire party driving down to Whites City, somebody can volunteer to drive down, allowing the rest of your group to take a great desert hike and warm up after the coolish visit to the depths of Carlsbad Caverns. If you're early for your cave trip, you can do this in reverse. One person drives up to the headquarters, and the rest of the party hikes up from Whites City.

From a geologist's perspective, this trail starts at the base of the Capitan Reef and climbs to the top where the caverns are located. From a hiker's perspective, it's an extra pleasant stroll through a desert environment.

From the west end, it's a very easy hike, but even if you start at Whites City, it's not difficult. You climb for about a half-mile and then, it's essentially flat the rest of the way to the amphitheater. Shortly up the trail from the Whites City Campground, you find a "walk only" gate to keep out motorized vehicles.

The trail is well-defined and easy to follow all the way with the exception of the uphill section at the east end. Here, the trail fades away in the rocks here and there, but you can find your way by following cairns and brown trail markers placed in strategic locations by the NPS.

From the top of the ridge, you get a good view of tiny Whites City below and the "great flat" beyond. Along the trail, you also get to see much of the desert vegetation you may have read about on the interpretive signs along the Chihuahuan Desert Nature Trail.

This trail traces the same route used by guano miners in the early 1900s to haul the prized fertilizer to Whites City in wagons. You can still see signs of the past, as two wagon tracks are visible much of the way. You can also see a few pieces of abandoned mining equipment rusting away along the abandoned road. Please do not remove any of this "garbage" left by guano miners. These historical artifacts have little value when removed, and in their current location, they become part of the fascinating story of guano mining. Preserve this story for other hikers to follow. (And besides, it's illegal to remove them for the park.)

3 JUNIPER RIDGE

Type of trail:	Out and back.
Type of trip:	Day hike.
Total distance:	2-4 miles.
Difficulty:	Easy.
Elevation change:	800 feet.
Time required:	1-2 hours.
Maps:	Trails Illustrated Carlsbad Caverns Map and USGS Carlsbad Caverns.
Starting point:	One mile past marker 15 on Scenic Loop Drive.

> **See Map on Page 27**

Finding the trailhead: The only difficult part of this trail is finding it. Take Scenic Loop Drive turnout off the paved road to park headquarters, just east of the visitor center. You must be careful not to miss it because you can't turn around and backtrack on this one-way road.

This trail used to be called "North Boundary Trail," so if you see any old handouts or signs, they actually refer to the Juniper Ridge Trail. The NPS handout might say the trail starts "just past" marker 15 on Scenic Loop Drive, but it actually starts about 1 mile past marker 15, almost to marker 16. There's no parking area at the trailhead. Set your odometer at marker 15 and go about 0.9 mile until you see a pullout on the north side of the road. Park here and walk about 200 yards up the road until you see the trail heading off to the north. If you see marker 16, park and walk back down the road to the trailhead. Watch for a sign at the trailhead as well as a faint trail and a string of cairns heading north from the road.

The trail: This is an ideal short hike to take during your afternoon drive around Scenic Loop Drive, perhaps after your visit to the cave earlier that morning. Unlike most other hikes in the park, however, the trail to the north boundary does not follow

a canyon bottom. Instead, it's a short walk in the desert and serves as a good introduction to desert hiking.

Another good plan is to take this hike early in the morning before the desert heats
up. This gives you a better chance the see wildlife and the gorgeous morning light
highlighting the desert landscape. Then, about the time the sun is bearing down hard,
you can head for the cool depths of the cave.

The trail is fairly easy to follow. It's well-defined in some places, not in others,
but in all cases, well-placed cairns show the way. With a few small switchbacks, the
trail heads north up a moderately steep upgrade for about a mile up to the fence line
which marks the park boundary.

You can turn back here making the total distance about 2 miles, and this is the
official end of the trail. However, you can stretch the hike out to about 4 miles by
following the fence line for awhile. You can go either left or right, but make a mental
picture of the spot where the trail meets the fence line.

The cairns continue along the fence line up to a mile in each direction. When,
cairns start to get scarce and hard to see, turn back. When you head back be careful you don't walk right by the trail going south to the trailhead and continue following cairns along the boundary. This is actually easy to do since much of the terrain
is strikingly similar.

This trail offers a good opportunity to sample the park's wildflowers and other
vegetation and to see wildlife, especially on early morning walks. On the way back
you get a nice view into the expansive Walnut Canyon, formed by the powerful flash
floods that roar down the canyon once every two or three years. You can also see
the canyon's namesake, undersized walnut trees, lining the streambed.

4   RATTLESNAKE CANYON

Type of trail:	Out and back or loop.
Type of trip:	Day hike or overnighter.
Total distance:	6 miles (out and back), 5 miles (loop).
Difficulty:	Moderate.
Elevation change:	670 feet (out and back), 440 feet (loop)
Time required:	3-4 hours.
Maps:	Trails Illustrated Carlsbad Caverns Map and USGS Ser-pentine Bends.
Starting point:	Marker 9 on Scenic Loop Drive.

Finding the trailhead: The trail starts at marker 9 on the Scenic Loop Drive, a well-
maintained gravel road that leaves the paved entrance road to the park just east of
the visitor center. This is a one-way road, so be careful not to be taken in by the
scenery and miss marker 9, as you'll have to drive all the way around again to get
to the trailhead. There's room to park three or four vehicles at marker 9.

The trail: This is definitely one of the most scenic and accessible trails in Carlsbad
Caverns. Yet, like most other surface trails in the park, you're likely to have the trail
all to yourself. Rattlesnake Canyon is a large, open valley where you can quietly soak

RATTLESNAKE CANYON

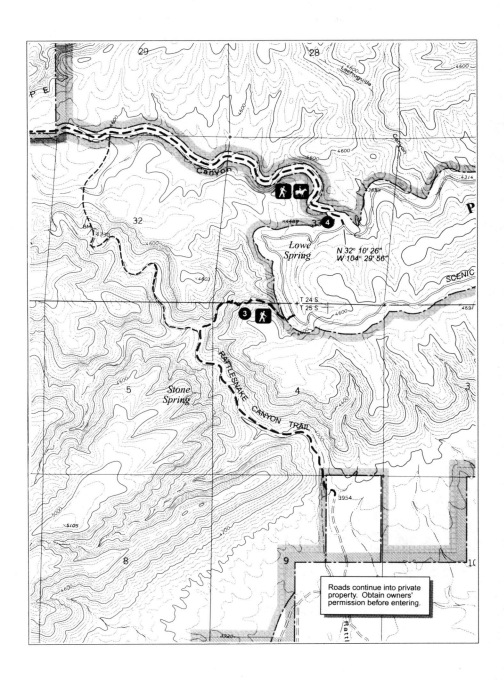

Roads continue into private property. Obtain owners' permission before entering.

Cairns are all that mark parts of the Rattlesnake Canyon Trail.

in the true essence of the Chihuahuan Desert and the rugged individuality of its plants and animals. If you plan to take a cave route, consider getting up early and hike Rattlesnake Canyon when the temperature is lower and the wildlife is out in force. Then, visit the cave in the afternoon.

When hiking Rattlesnake Canyon, you have two options. You can follow the canyon out to the park boundary and return to the trailhead, or you can take a small loop by connecting with the Guadalupe Ridge Trail and following it back to Scenic Loop Drive, coming out about a mile up the road from the Rattlesnake Canyon Trailhead. If you opt for the loop option and have two vehicles in your party, leave one at the Guadalupe Ridge Trailhead.

Both the loop and the out-and-back trip make excellent day hikes, but you can also make Rattlesnake Canyon an overnight trip. You can, of course, do this loop in reverse, but this description describes the clockwise route.

At the beginning, the trail is slightly confusing. From the parking area, it goes off to the right and down a short, steep hill to the bottom of the canyon. Then, it climbs briefly and traverses the left side of a small canyon for a short way. The first part of the trail is well-defined and easy to follow. Then, it drops down into the bottom of Rattlesnake Canyon and alternates between short sections of trail and stretches of dry wash with cairns showing the way. After the short descent into the bottom of the canyon, the trail remains fairly level the rest of the way.

Rattlesnake is a wide-open and more vegetatively diverse canyon than others in the park. Some of the broad, flat benches are almost like grassland. There's lots of deer food—and lots of deer.

About 1.5 miles into Rattlesnake Canyon, you hit a signed junction. The loop trail (marked "Guadalupe Ridge") veers off to the right and heads west up North Rattlesnake Canyon and then north over a small ridge and down to the Guadalupe Ridge Trail. This recently opened trail is defined most of the way with cairns marking the sections where the trail gets faint.

You can also hike straight along the canyon (marked "Stone Ranch") for about 2 miles to the park boundary and return to the trailhead. Just past the point where the new trail heads up to Guadalupe Ridge, you pass through historic Stone Ranch. Stone Springs (up the hill to the right) provided water for an early 1900s ranch in Rattlesnake Canyon. You can scramble up to see the springs, but it's a steep climb. You can see some old evidence of the ranching operations at both the springs and in the canyon along the trail.

If you plan to stay overnight, try to find a good campsite somewhere along the canyon floor, perhaps on one of the delightful grassy benches that line the lower canyon south of Stone Springs Ranch. After a pleasant night in the desert, you can take the short hike back to the trailhead or the loop route. The elevation gain back to the trailhead on both routes is about the same.

To take the loop option, go right when you juncture with the Guadalupe Ridge Trail and hike gradually downhill along Walnut Canyon for about 2 miles to Scenic Loop Drive. If you don't have a shuttle vehicle at the end of the hike, somebody will have to volunteer to hike the extra mile along Scenic Loop Drive to the Rattlesnake Canyon Trailhead to get your vehicle.

5 GUADALUPE RIDGE

> **Type of trail:** Out and back.
> **Type of trip:** Day hike or overnighter.
> **Total distance:** 27 miles to west boundary and back, but shorter hikes are possible.
> **Difficulty:** Easy to difficult, depending on distance.
> **Elevation change:** 2,050 feet.
> **Time required:** Depends on distance hiked, 10-15 hours to park boundary and back.
> **Maps:** Trails Illustrated Carlsbad Caverns Map, USGS Serpentine Bends, Gunsight Canyon, and Queen.
> **Starting point:** The well-marked trailhead on Scenic Loop Drive.

Key points:

- 2.0 Rattlesnake Canyon Trail Junction.
- 2.5 First gate.
- 2.9 Walnut Creek dry wash.
- 3.0 Second gate.
- 7.0 Slaughter Ridge Trail Junction.
- 9.5 Slaughter Canyon Trail Junction.
- 11.7 Putman Cabin.
- 11.8 Park Boundary.

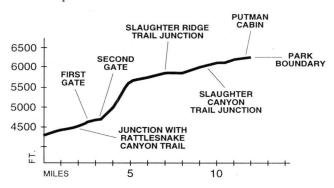

Finding the trailhead: The trail starts about halfway around Scenic Loop Drive, a well-maintained gravel road that leaves the paved entrance road to the park just east of the visitor center. This is a one-way road, so be careful not to miss the sign that says "Guadalupe Ridge Trail." If you have a low-clearance vehicle, it's best to park here. You can drive your four-wheeler the first 2.5 miles, but it's such a pleasant walk, it's hard to figure why anybody would want to bump and grind up the road in a vehicle. After a gate about 2.5 miles up the trail, the road deteriorates badly, and vehicle use is not advised.

The trail: The Guadalupe Ridge Trail is the center stage of the Carlsbad Caverns trail system. From this trail, you can see most of the park, and get a great feeling for the expansiveness and beauty of Carlsbad Caverns above the surface. You can also hike parts of the ridge trail on the Rattlesnake Canyon Loop and the Slaughter Canyon Loop. Since the Guadalupe Ridge Trail is a mostly abandoned jeep road, the NPS allows mountain biking. However, mountain biking off this trail is strictly prohibited, either cross-country or on connecting trails down Rattlesnake or Slaughter canyons.

Like all desert hiking, it's best to go early. Walnut Canyon is always a grand place to hike, but it's even better at first light. You're likely to see deer and other desert wildlife during the first hours of daylight.

The first 3 miles follow Walnut Canyon and is easy walking. You go through two gates, as the trail goes out and then, a 0.5 mile later, back into the park. The public has legal access to this Bureau of Land Management land, but be sure to close the gates. You cross the usually dry streambed of Walnut Creek just after the second gate.

There is a slight chance you might see a jeep driving the road, but this is very rare. The road is very rough and tough on vehicles, and the towing expense can be astronomical.

Walnut is bigger and more open than most canyons in the park. Watch for wildlife, which is abundant, especially a healthy population of mule deer. Golden eagles often soar through the canyon looking for a black-tailed jackrabbit for dinner. And if you're out at daybreak, you might see a ringtail. Also, the wildflower show is sensational along the first section of the trail.

Right after the second gate, the trail heads up a steep hill and keeps climbing for about 3 miles until you reach the top of the ridge. From that point on, you face only small ups and downs, and the trail stays essentially level or slightly uphill to the west boundary and Putman Cabin.

Although it's a healthy climb to get to the top of the ridge, it's still easier than going up Slaughter Canyon or Yucca Canyon trails to reach the same elevation. The trail, which is an unmaintained jeep road, is much easier to walk than most trails. You can spend your time gazing at the spectacular scenery instead of making sure you have the next cairn spotted. If you want to make good time, you're on the right trail. You can average 2-3 mph on this trail, where you are hard-pressed to do 1.5 mph on most park trails.

This trail offers a variety of hiking. If you're out for a pleasant early morning or late evening stroll, you can walk all or part of the first 3 miles and return to your vehicle. If you want to stay out one or two nights, you're also on the right trail. Once you get to the top of the ridge, you'll find several excellent places to camp. Probably the best camping areas are in a juniper grove around the junction with Slaughter Canyon trail, which heads off to the west at about the 9.5-mile mark.

From the ridge, you see some of the best scenery in the park. This could be called "reef-walking" as you're right on top of the 250-million-year-old Capitan Reef. There's no El Capitan or Grand Teton or Longs Peak around to dominate the landscape. Instead, you look down in one canyon after another as they end near the ridgeline.

You can see Putman Cabin and its big antenna a long way off sitting on top of a high point in the ridge. The cabin isn't the stereotypical old log cabin you might visualize when look at the map, but it does have an outdoor toilet you can use.

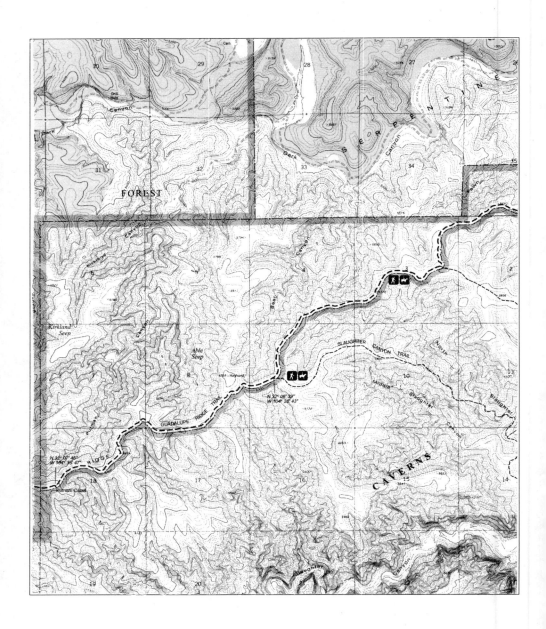

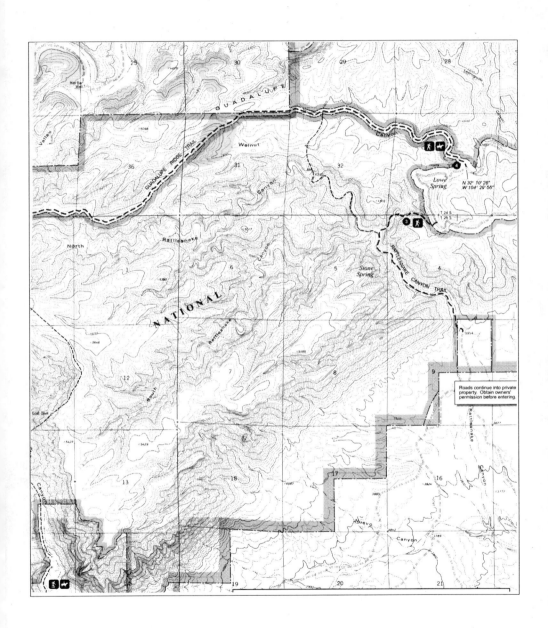

Roads continue into private
property. Obtain owners'
permission before entering.

N 32° 10' 26"
W 104° 29' 55"

If you're retracing your steps on the ridge, you can see Carlsbad Caverns Head-quarters many miles away, but you don't have to walk quite that far. The last few miles back to park headquarters are part of Scenic Loop Drive.

You can also make this a shuttle hike by leaving a vehicle or arranging to be picked up at the Slaughter Canyon Trailhead. If you take this option, you don't have to retrace your steps to Scenic Loop Drive. And you can drop your pack and take a short side trip over to Putman Cabin and the west boundary before heading down Slaughter Canyon.

You can reach Slaughter Canyon Trailhead on two different trails. The first option (signed junction at the 7-mile mark) goes along Slaughter Ridge before steeply dropping into broad and beautiful Slaughter Canyon. The second route (signed junction at the 9.5-mile mark) follows the ridge between North and Middle Slaughter canyons for about 1.5 miles before dropping (not quite as steeply) in the canyon bottom.

6 SLAUGHTER CANYON

Type of trail: Out and back, loop, or shuttle.
Type of trip: Day hike or overnighter.
Total distance: 14 miles
Difficulty: Difficult.
Elevation change: 1,850 feet.
Time required: 8-10 hours.
Maps: Trails Illustrated Carlsbad Caverns Map and USGS Serpentine Bends and Grapevine Draw.
Starting point: Parking lot for Slaughter Canyon Cave (may be called "New Cave" in older publications)

Key points:
- 1.5 West Slaughter Canyon.
- 3.0 Junction with Slaughter Ridge Trail.
- 5.5 Junction with Guadalupe Ridge Trail.
- 8.0 Junction with Slaughter Ridge Trail.
- 11.0 Junction with main trail up Slaughter Canyon.
- 14.0 Slaughter Canyon Trailhead.

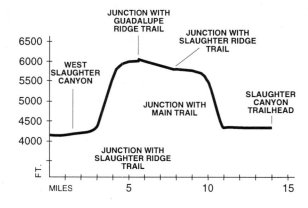

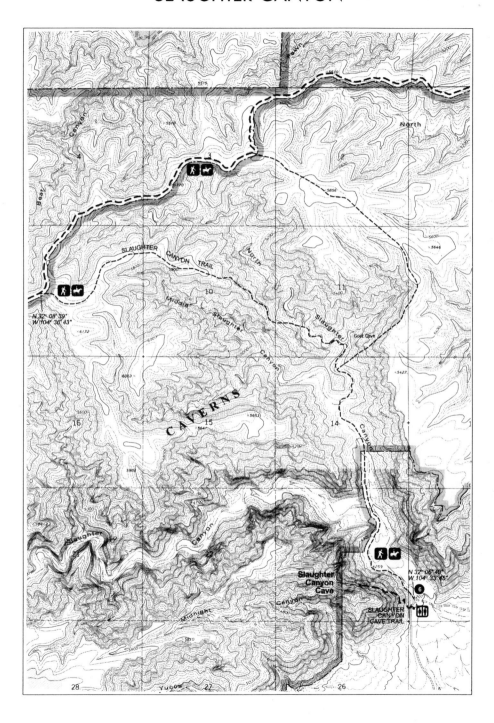

Slaughter Canyon Trail.

Finding the trailhead: The paved road to Slaughter Canyon Cave (County Road 418) turns off U.S. Highway 62/180, 6 miles south of Whites City. The signs at the turnoff say "Slaughter Canyon Cave" and "Washington Ranch." Follow County Road 418 for 10 miles until you reach the park boundary and the road turns to gravel. Follow the gravel road for another mile until it deadends at the trailhead. There is plenty of parking at the trailhead, which also has toilet and picnic facilities.

The trail: Slaughter Canyon is a broad desert canyon with three major branches—West, Middle, and North. Get out the long pants for this trail. It gets brushy, and your desert friends—catclaw, sotol, cholla, and their thorny relatives—can torture bare legs.

Slaughter Canyon offers many options. It can be a leisurely day hike of 2 to 3 miles up the fairly level canyon and then returning to the trailhead, or you can make it a fitness test by tackling the entire 14-mile loop in a single, long day.

However, Slaughter Canyon is probably best suited to a backpacking adventure with one or two nights out in the remote desert wilderness. You can also make this part of a long shuttle hike by starting at the Guadalupe Ridge Trailhead on Scenic Loop Drive and ending at the Slaughter Canyon Trailhead.

Two trails leave from this trailhead, so the first order of business is to make sure you're on the right one. Don't take the lefthand trail to Slaughter Canyon Cave, which is more heavily used and defined than the Slaughter Canyon Trail. The correct trail is just to the right of the cave trail. The sign at the trailhead refers to the trail as the "Middle Slaughter Canyon Trail." The cave trail immediately starts climbing, and the canyon trail stays low and follows the dry wash.

The trail starts out on a beautiful grassy bench and then winds in and out of the canyon wash. Watch carefully for cairns along this stretch as it's easy to miss them in places. A few sections of the trail don't have enough cairns, but don't fret. The trail continues up the canyon wash. If you stay in the canyon wash, you'll get to the same place as the trail goes, but staying on the trail is easier on the feet and makes the trip slightly shorter, as it cuts across some of the meanders.

You might see spur trails heading off to the left or right. Ignore these and keep heading up the main canyon. About 1.5 miles up the trail, you can see West Slaughter Canyon heading off to the left.

The gradual incline up Slaughter Canyon continues for 3 miles at which point, you see a sign indicating the start of the loop trail. The right fork goes up to Slaughter Ridge, and the left fork climbs up to a ridge between North Slaughter Canyon and Middle Slaughter Canyon. You can take this loop either way, of course, but clockwise is easier because you can avoid the extremely steep ascent up to Slaughter Ridge.

If you've planned two nights out, you might want to find a campsite somewhere along the canyon floor around this junction. If you plan only one night out, you should continue up to Guadalupe Ridge and camp along the ridge trail or just before you get there on the ridge between North and Middle Slaughter canyons.

After turning left at this junction, you start climbing. This is difficult hiking, especially with an overnight pack. It's steep, and the trail fades away in a few places where you must follow well-placed cairns. After a tough mile, the steep climb is behind you, and you hike on a fairly level trail along the ridge. The vistas from the ridgeline are fantastic.

When you reach the Guadalupe Ridge Trail, you can drop your pack and take a short side trip over to Putman Cabin. It's about 2 miles to the left (west) along the ridge trail. If you camp near the junction of Slaughter Canyon and Guadalupe Ridge Trail, the side trip to Putman Cabin would be perfect for a late evening or early morning stroll.

After your overnight stay, take a right (east) down the Guadalupe Ridge Trail for 2.5 miles until you see a sign indicating the newly opened section of trail along Slaughter Ridge. Take a right (south) here and follow the fairly level trail for another 2.5 miles until it drops abruptly down to the bottom of the main Slaughter Canyon. From here retrace your steps back to the trailhead.

7 YUCCA CANYON

Type of trip: Out and back.
Type of trail: Day hike or overnighter.
Total distance: 7 miles to the top of Yucca Canyon and back; 12 miles to the head of Double Canyon and back.
Difficulty: Difficult.
Elevation change: 1,520 feet.
Time required: 6-8 hours.
Maps: Trails Illustrated Carlsbad Caverns Map, USGS Grapevine Draw and Gunsight Canyon.
Starting point: Yucca Canyon Trailhead.

YUCCA CANYON

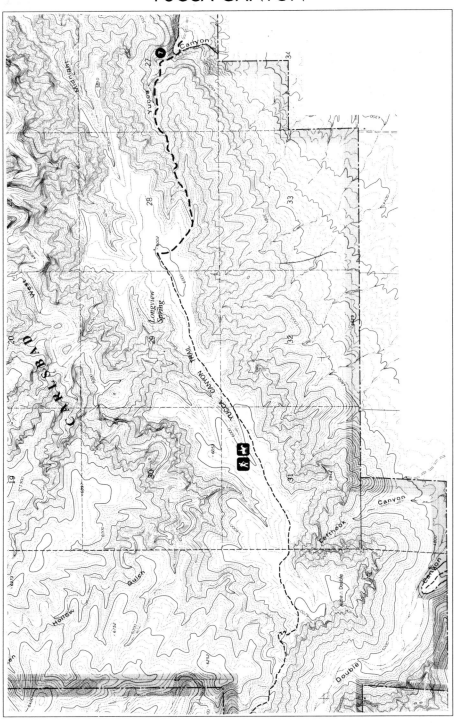

View from top of Yucca Canyon.

Key points:
    3.5 Top of ridge.
    4.0 Turn off to Longview Spring.
    5.0 Lefthook Canyon.
    6.0 End of trail.

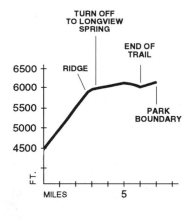

Finding the trailhead: The paved road to the Yucca Canyon Trailhead (County Road 418) turns off U.S. Highway 62/180, 6 miles south of Whites City. The signs at the turnoff say "Slaughter Canyon Cave" and "Washington Ranch." Follow County 418 for 10 miles until you reach the park boundary and the road turns to gravel. At this point, turn left (west) onto a rough gravel road that follows the north side of the fence line. Stay on this road for 1.7 miles until it ends at the Yucca Canyon Trailhead. You should have a high-clearance vehicle for the last 1.7 miles, but you can make it, barely, with a low-clearance vehicle.

The trail: This is, perhaps, the most dramatic and scenic trail in the park. It might also be the most rugged.

Yucca Canyon is suited for a long day hike or an overnighter. If you day hike, get up early and plan on getting back late. If you backpack, you can spend the night up on the ridge above Yucca Canyon. This is a special treat, but you have to earn it. It's a rough uphill grind (more than 1,500 feet in about 3.5 miles!) with a overnight pack to get there. Staying overnight gives you the time to do several splendid side trips in the area.

Most canyon hikes in the park, such as Slaughter Canyon just to the east, at least start out with a near-level walk along the streambed, but not in this case. You start climbing right from the trailhead.

This is a narrower, more scenic canyon than others in the park. The scenery is so absorbing that you might forget the steady elevation gain. The vegetation is so diverse and lush (but no more yucca than other canyons) that you might think the canyon has a spring-fed stream, but no water is visible.

You'll also see one precipitous rock formation after another. In two places, the cliffs on both sides of the canyon come together like gates.

The trail is very well-constructed and defined—perhaps the best in the park. The climbing ends after about 3.5 miles when you reach the top of the escarpment and break out into a gorgeous grove of junipers with a grassy carpet, perhaps the closest thing to a forest you'll find in this park.

From here, the hiking is fairly flat. Up here, the trail is less defined, but still easy to follow because of a steady string of cairns. The trail turns west and wanders through the junipers for about a mile. It's easy to feel lonely up here. It seems like you have a whole wilderness to yourself and the only sounds are the wind making music as it sifts through the junipers and an occasional deer bounding away.

If you were wondering about that strange green spot on the USGS topo map, you're in it. The green generally follows the boundaries of the juniper grove. This isn't the only spot like this in the park and, in fact, there are other spots with as much or more vegetation, but for some reason, the USGS chose to highlight this juniper grove.

The cliffs of Double Canyon at the end of the Yucca Canyon hike.

If you're staying overnight, you'll want to pick a choice campsite amid the junipers. You may see a fenced enclosure where the NPS is conducting a vegetation study, and you might also see a small shanty that serves as a patrol cabin for park rangers. Stay clear of the cabin when setting up your camp.

If you're day hiking, you might want to have a long lunch in the junipers and head back. However, if you're ambitious, you can continue along the ridge overlooking Double Canyon, about another 2.5 miles (one way).

As you approach Double Canyon, the trail gets harder to find, and you must rely completely on cairns in most places. But it stays level as you walk the ridgeline, and the scenery is fantastic all the way.

About a mile before Double canyon, you can peek over the cliffs into precipitous Lefthook Canyon. Another mile down the trail gives you a similar view into the much larger Double Canyon. Both canyons veer off to the south from the ridge.

Shortly after your view over the sheer cliffs into Double Canyon, the trail takes a sharp turn to the left (south) and heads down a short hill to a saddle at the head of Double Canyon. At this point the trail more or less disappears. The USGS and Trails Illustrated maps show the trail continuing out the west end of the park and connecting with Guadalupe Ridge several miles into the Lincoln National Forest. But on the ground the trail is barely visible with a few scattered cairns marking the way.

If you're an ambitious and experienced hiker, you can turn left and follow a level rock ledge for about 0.5 mile. From this point, you can look off to the east side of Double Canyon and see the spectacular "Double Cliffs" you were able to peek over when you were on the ridgeline trail a few minutes earlier. You also get a great view of expansive Double Canyon. This side trip can be dangerous, so be careful.

After a good rest at the end of the trail, retrace your steps back to the juniper grove at the top of Yucca Canyon.

Another nice side trip from the juniper grove at the head of Yucca Canyon is the short cross-country trip to Longview Springs. You'll need your compass and topo map, but it isn't hard to find. If you get lucky, you'll be able to follow well-defined deer trails to the spring. From the spring, you definitely get a "long view" off to the west. The spring is merely a seep with not much water flow, but nonetheless, it's a wonderful oasis in the desert. Don't plan on using the spring for drinking water, and be extra careful not to trample sensitive plants around the springs.

On the way back down Yucca Canyon, you'll be quickly reminded how steep it was getting up. You might have been reveling in the scenery and not noticed. It's so steep that it's hard to walk down in places.

THE GRAND CREATION

Water, from oceans to tiny droplets, has created and shaped Carlsbad Cavern. The rocks in which the cavern formed are the product of an ancient reef that flourished 250 million years ago during the Permian period. The water was warm, and near the shore was a favorable place for a host of marine lime-secreting plants and animals to live.

Generation followed generation, and limy remains of the plants and animals, along with lime (calcium carbonate) that precipitated from the water, built up a reef along the edge of the inland sea. For millions of years as the entire region subsided, the reef grew upward and outward, maintaining a height just below sea level.

Eventually the reef was hundreds of feet thick and 1 to 4 miles across. Behind the reef, on the tidal flats and in the lagoon behind them, limestone and occasional sandstone sheets were deposited at about the same rate the reef was growing. On the seaward side, chunks of limestone broke away and tumbled down from the steep seaward face of the growing reef. These broken pieces of rock formed an underwater talus slope or rubble pile. The upper level of Carlsbad Cavern is in the thin layered back reef and tidal flat deposits, while the large chambers and lower levels are in the reef and reef talus deposits.

Eventually the channels supplying water from the ocean slowly closed, and the sea began to dry up. The water evaporated more rapidly than it was replaced. Salts and gypsum were precipitated and filled the basin.

In time, the basin was no more. The landscape was a nearly flat surface, with little relief. As eons passed, the old sea basin, the reef, and the surrounding regions were deeply buried under additional thousands of feet of sediments.

Starting with its burial and continuing as movement began to occur in more recent times, fractures developed in the old reef and overlying deposits. As the Guadalupe Mountains were first raised by compressive earth movements (20 to 40 million years ago), fresh water filled some of the fractures. Fresh ground water mixed with briney waters, saturating the basin-filling rocks, increasing the solubility of limestones. Sulfurous gasses, seeping upwards from far below and present in the brines, were oxidized to sulfuric acid and contributed to the processes of limestone dissolution.

Slowly—ever so slowly—these processes dissolved the adjacent limestone. Slow movements of the water carried the dissolved material away. This process of dissolving and removing continued over extreme lengths of time. The eventual result was a honeycomb of openings filled with water. The largest chambers in the cave occur at three levels (200, 750, and 830 feet) below the present surface. Probably the water table remained static at these levels, so more time was available for dissolving the limestone.

Finally, 2 to 4 million years ago, massive earth movements again uplifted and tilted the entire region with the higher area to the west. Erosion stripped away the overlying sediments. The limestone of the exposed fossil reef was much harder than the basin salts and gypsum. The old reef was much more resistant to erosion, and today the edge of the old sea basin is well marked by the ridge that extends from near the city of Carlsbad southwestward to Guadalupe Peak.

As uplift continued, ground water drained away leaving air-filled openings. With the loss of buoyancy that the ground water had supplied, many massive chunks of weakened rock could not support their own weight and collapse was commonplace, thus leaving large underground chambers and passageways. The basic shape of the cavern was fairly well defined by this time.

Massive deposits of gypsum are present in several locations in Carlsbad Cavern. While it is believed that the gypsum was brought into the cavern in solution, it is not yet clear just how or when the material was deposited.

Decoration of the cave began as chambers became air-filled. Even when lower parts of the chamber were still flooded, decoration began in the drained upper portions. Again, water is nature's primary tool in this process, which is still going on. Rain and snow water percolating through the soil picks up a small amount of carbon dioxide from organic material and becomes a weak acid. Each drop can dissolve a tiny bit of limestone and carry it along on its downward trip. When the droplet reaches the air-filled chamber, some carbon dioxide escapes into the cave air, and the water's ability to hold limestone in solution is reduced. A tiny part of the limestone that was carried in is then precipitated from the water and left on the ceiling, wall, or floor of the chamber again as limestone or as calcite crystals. Drop after drop, depositing particle after particle, the cavern decorations are created.

Even though water has been the instrument of creation and decoration in Carlsbad Cavern, there is no evidence that any major flowing streams contributed to its formation, although some minor streams may have followed a few passageways. There are areas where ponds have formed and stood for long periods of time. Some still exist today but they are very small. Green Lake, Mirror Lake and others are just a few feet across. Among the larger cavern pools is Lake of the Clouds, which lies at the lowest known point in Carlsbad Cavern.

Lake of the Clouds is located nearly 0.5 mile away from the nearest public trail and at the bottom of a very steep-sided pit. The surface elevation of this small lake is over 1,000 feet below the natural entrance. It is 11-feet deep, has no apparent drainage, and its level remains nearly constant.

There is no way of telling the exact age of any cave formation. The rate of growth depends on several variables such as water supply, rate of flow, amount of material carried, and other factors that can change drastically from place to place as well as from time to time.

Reprinted with permission from Carlsbad Caverns:
Silent Chambers, Timeless Beauty published by
The Carlsbad Caverns-Guadalupe Mountains Association

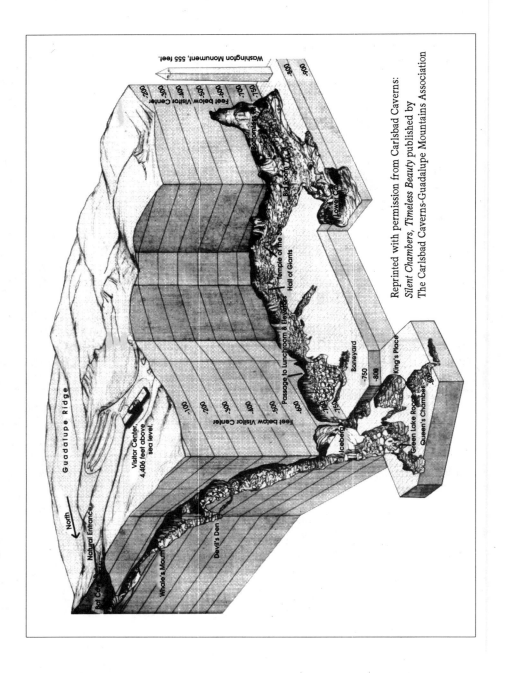

Reprinted with permission from Carlsbad Caverns:
Silent Chambers, Timeless Beauty published by
The Carlsbad Caverns-Guadalupe Mountains Association

CAVE ROUTES

At Carlsbad Caverns National Park, the National Park Service has put together a spectacular and diverse package of cave routes for park visitors. Park visitors can choose from eight cave routes ranging from very easy to very difficult.

It would be much easier for the NPS to herd everybody through the caverns on the self-guided tours. But instead, they provide the opportunity for "wild cave experiences."

The ultra-popular self-guided tours still attract most visitors, just as they have for decades. But in recent years the NPS has added ranger-led trips to the selection. Two of these ranger-led tours are fairly easy, but two of the cave routes are nothing short of a down-and-dirty caving experiences. Here's the line-up, listed in approximate order of difficulty:

SELF-GUIDED TOURS:

    Big Room
    Natural Entrance

CAVING EXPERIENCES:

    Spider Cave
    Hall of the White Giant

GUIDED TOURS:

    King's Palace
    Lefthand Tunnel
    Lower Cave
    Slaughter Canyon Cave

For all routes, you definitely need good hiking shoes. Don't show up in sandals, high heels or shoes with slick soles. Also, to really enjoy the cave, bring a good flashlight (and extra batteries). Small, weak flashlights don't allow you to clearly see the fantastic formations. Parents should carefully supervise young children, and for safety reasons, the NPS does not allow strollers in the cave.

For the caving trips, you need a special piece of equipment—courage. These trips are not for the faint-hearted. They are, in fact, an introduction to the sport of caving. They also require at least a moderate level of physical fitness.

One note of caution—big people beware. Anybody the size of an NFL lineman should avoid the Spider Cave and Hall of the White Giant. On these two trips, you not only get down on your belly and crawl through the mud, but you also have to squeeze through some spaces tight enough to bring out deep-rooted claustrophobic tendencies.

You also need old clothes. The NPS hands out a hard-hat with light along with knee and elbow pads at the start of the trip.

Because of the physical difficulty of the off-trail cave routes, the NPS discourages children under age 12 from signing up. Also, people who have difficulty with low levels of light, small spaces, or heights may prefer the self-guided tours. Many parts of these off-trail trips are physically demanding, wet and slippery, and have tight squeezes, and at times require handlines (short, fixed ropes) to get up steep slopes. All off-trail tours have a special "blackout" to truly experience the natural cave.

Up on the surface, the hiking is free. But the NPS charges a small fee for the cave routes. (Sorry, Golden Eagle Passports do not apply. Holders of the Golden Age or Golden Access passports get a 50 percent discount.) You must make reservations for all tours except the two self-guided routes. Call 1-505-785-2232 ext. 429 any time between 8:30 a.m. and 4:30 p.m. MST for reservations. If you are unable to keep your reservations, please notify the park within 24 hours to receive a full refund. This courtesy allows others to take these limited-participation tours.

NOTE: Even though the current schedules are included in the following descriptions, be sure to call in advance and double check, as all schedules are subject to change. As a special courtesy to rangers and others on your trip, try to arrive a few minutes early.

NECESSARY EQUIPMENT

• Good walking shoes—no high heels, sandals, or shoes with slick soles.

• Sweater, sweatshirt, or light coat. The cave stays a constant temperature of 56 degrees Fahrenheit which might seem chilly compared to the 90 degree + of the desert above.

• Good flashlight with extra batteries.

FOR EVERYBODY

For safety reasons and to preserve the cave experience for many generations to come, the NPS has imposed a few rules for all underground routes.

• No smoking allowed anywhere in any caves in Carlsbad Caverns National Park, including the Underground Lunch Room.

• Stay on designated trails at all times.

• Do not touch any cave formations.

• Keep children under close supervision at all times.

• Do not flash other cave visitors with your camera.

• No strollers allowed anywhere in Carlsbad Caverns.

• Try to be as quiet as possible to preserve the cave experience for other visitors.

• Never throw anything in cave pools.

• Do not bring food or beverage into caves.

1 NATURAL ENTRANCE

Type of trail: Self-guided tour on a paved path.
Schedule: Any time between 8:30 a.m. and 3:30 p.m. daily from May through August and 8:30 a.m. to 2 p.m. September through April. No reservations required. Buy tickets at the visitor center.
Special regulations: No strollers. Stay on cave trails at all times.
Total distance: 1 mile—plus and additional 1 mile if you go through the Big Room.
Difficulty: Moderate. Not recommended for anyone with heart, breathing, or walking difficulties.
Time required: 1 hour—or 2 hours if you add the Big Room route.
Starting point: Visitor center.

Finding the trailhead: To find the trailhead, turn west off U.S. Highway 62/180 at Whites City (20 miles south of Carlsbad, New Mexico) and drive 7 miles on a paved road to the park headquarters and visitor center.

The trail: Assuming you're physically ready for a steep, 2-mile, mostly downhill walk, the natural entrance route probably gets the nod as the best way to see Carlsbad Caverns. You get the spine-tingling sensation of descending 75 stories into the Big Room and from there, you can take the Big Room route, and then, you can avoid climbing back up by taking the elevator to the surface. What a deal!

Heading into the Natural Entrance.

Before you leave the visitor center, rent a hand-held radio receiver that automatically gives you transmitted messages at key points along the way. You'll also find many excellent interpretive signs along the way to explain the story of Carlsbad Caverns.

As you leave the visitor center and start down the long, winding path to the Natural Entrance, try to imagine what it was like for those who discovered the cave. Local Indians were the first to enter the cave, but they probably did not go into its depths.

In the late 1800s, local cowboys noticed "smoke" coming out of a hole in the ground. But when they went to investigate that cloud of smoke, it turned out to be millions of bats leaving the cave at dusk. Bats still inhabit the cave, but the population has been much reduced by use of insecticides and early damage to their critical cave habitat. The bats roost in a section of the cave closed off from public access, so you probably won't see any bats on your trip into the cave. However, you might see cave swallows darting here and there around the Natural Entrance. If you want to see bats (and it's quite the spectacle!) make sure you take a seat at the Bat Flight Amphitheater at the Natural Entrance at dusk on any summer night.

After descending about 200 feet into the cave, you'll enter "The Twilight Zone," the mysterious region of a cave that still gets faint light from the outside world, but is mostly dominated by the blackness of the cavern depths. Past the Twilight Zone, you see the cave with the help of more than 1,000 light bulbs and 19 miles of wire, all esthetically and carefully placed by the NPS to enhance the cave experience. It may seem like the NPS used colored lights, but instead, the NPS strategically places lights to highlight the natural colors of the cave formations. (And yes, there is a back-up lighting system in case of a power outage.)

In Carlsbad Caverns, the temperature stays at a comfortable 56 degrees F, regardless of how hot or humid it gets outside. The temperature and humidity of the surface does, however, affect the air flow in and out of the cave, so you might notice a slight cave wind blowing or "breathing," as the NPS calls it.

As you continue down through a section called the Devil's Den, imagine how it must have been descending into the depths without the nicely contoured pathway. That's how many park visitors experienced the caverns in the early 1900s.

After about a mile of walking back and forth on the endless series of switchbacks, you come across the famous Iceberg Rock. This gigantic rock (weighing an estimated 200,000 tons!) fell from the ceiling. This was a "big bang" that nobody heard.

Shortly after Iceberg Rock you reach a junction where you can go left to the Underground Lunch Room, elevators, and rest rooms or you can continue on and take the Big Room route.

You've now had your mile-long descent into Carlsbad Caverns. You can call it a day and take elevators to the surface, but if you do, you'll miss the best part of a trip to Carlsbad Caverns, the Big Room.

2 THE BIG ROOM

             Type of trail: Self-guided tour on a paved path.
                 Schedule: Any time between 8:30 a.m. and 3:30 p.m. daily from
                               May through August and 8:30 a.m. to 2 p.m. September
                               through April. No reservations required. Buy tickets at
                               the visitor center.
    Special regulations: No strollers. Stay on cave trails at all times.
          Total distance: 1.2 mile.
               Difficulty: Easy.
          Time required: 1-2 hours.
          Starting point: Visitor center.

Finding the trailhead: To find the trailhead, turn west off U.S. Highway 62\180 at Whites City (20 miles south of Carlsbad, New Mexico) and drive 7 miles on a paved road to the park headquarters and visitor center.

The trail: The Big Room route is the easiest way to see the wonders of Carlsbad Caverns. Since you take the elevator down to the Underground Lunch Room, where the trip starts and ends, the mile-long walk is largely level all the way. You can also extend the Natural Entrance route through the Big Room. A portion of the Big Room route is accessible to visitors using wheelchairs.

Before you jump on the elevator, rent a hand-held radio receiver that automatically turns off and on during the walk to explain the history and geology of the cave and specific features along the route. The nicely paved route is also lined with superb interpretive displays with much of the information duplicated from the tape. And rangers station themselves at key points along the way to answer questions.

They don't call it the Big Room for nothing. Many of the 82 known caves in Carlsbad Caverns National Park have large chambers, but the Big Room is the biggest of them all. The 14-acre chamber could encompass fourteen football fields, and the ceiling is 255 feet high. This is the home of the giant speleothems, especially those found in the Hall of Giants where you can find a 62-foot stalagmite called Giant Dome.

The Big Room also contains the small, elegant formations that compliment the huge pillars, making the Big Room a "must see" experience. The awe-inspiring expansiveness of the Big Room contains an incredible diversity of cave formations that reflect the fragile and timeless beauty of caves.

3 KING'S PALACE

Type of trail:	Ranger-guided tour on a paved path.
Schedule:	Daily at 9:00 a.m., 11:00 a.m., 1:00 p.m. and 3:00 p.m. Reservations required. Call 1-505-785-2232 ext. 429 for reservations, which require a VISA or MASTERCARD.
Special regulations:	No strollers. Stay on cave trails at all times.
Total distance:	About 0.5 mile.
Difficulty:	Moderate.
Time required:	About one hour.
Starting point:	At the Underground Lunch Room, a short elevator ride from the visitor center.

Finding the trailhead: To find the trailhead, turn west off U.S. Highway 62/180 at Whites City (20 miles south of Carlsbad, New Mexico) and drive 7 miles on a paved road to the park headquarters and visitor center.

The trail: The King's Palace route used to be part of the Natural Entrance self-guided route. However, some irreplaceable formations along the route were damaged by irresponsible visitors. To prevent further damage, the NPS turned the King's Palace trip into a ranger-guided tour in 1992.

The trip starts in the Underground Lunch Room where the ranger spends a few minutes summarizing the tour and preparing visitors for the trip. Then, the ranger leads you down a paved path (similar to the Natural Entrance trail) to new depths.

The King's Palace Route goes through the "scenic rooms" such as the King's Palace, the Queen's Chamber, and the Papoose Room. The scenic rooms have many fantastic cave features, all nicely interpreted by the ranger guiding the trip.

You keep switchbacking down until you reach a gorgeous cave pool called Green Lake. At this point, you're 830 feet below the surface, the deepest point of this trip. That's the equivalent of an 83-story building.

Beyond Green Lake, you gradually climb back up to the level of the Big Room where the route ends.

4 LEFTHAND TUNNEL

Type of trail:	Off-trail ranger-guided tour.
Schedule:	1 p.m. on Tuesday/Thursday. Call ahead (1-505-785-2232 ext. 429) for reservations, which require a VISA or MASTERCARD.
Special regulations:	Be sure you have good hiking boots or sturdy walking shoes. Stay on cave trails at all times. Limited to 25 people.
Total distance:	About 0.5 mile.
Difficulty:	Easy.
Time required:	1-2 hours.
Starting point:	Visitor center.

Finding the trailhead: To find the trailhead, turn west off U.S. Highway 62/180 at Whites City (20 miles south of Carlsbad, New Mexico) and drive 7 miles on a paved road to the park headquarters and visitor center.

The trail: The Lefthand Tunnel trip adds another perspective to the caving experience. It's an off-trail trip, but it's easier than Lower Cave and a walk in the park compared to Spider Cave and Hall of the White Giant. On these wilder routes, you're crawling around in the dirt and mud with a head lamp on your hard-hat. On the Lefthand Tunnel route, you use a designated path where you can walk upright the entire way with only lanterns for light.

You start the trip right in the Underground Lunch Room. At the far end, you go through a rustic old door that immediately sets the historic theme of the trip. You travel through a moderately large tunnel lit only by the dim light of candle lanterns similar to those used by early explorers.

The pale light of the lantern immediately starts you thinking of what it must have been like for the first explorers who braved the depths of Carlsbad Caverns without modern lights or knowledgeable rangers guiding the way. At the turnaround point, the rangers have a blackout and tell stories of the early explorations of Carlsbad Caverns.

The trip has some crystal clear cave pools and lots of examples of fossils in the rocks along the way. It lacks the awe-inspiring formations of other cave routes, but the trip has a special quality of getting you in the right frame of mind. You leave Lefthand Tunnel feeling quite fortunate to have modern conveniences and the NPS to take care of you and Carlsbad Caverns.

5 SLAUGHTER CANYON CAVE

Type of trail:	Ranger-guided tour on undeveloped trail in the cave, plus a short, steep (500-foot elevation gain) hike to the cave entrance.
Schedule:	Twice daily (10 a.m. and 2 p.m.) May through August, but only on Saturday and Sunday during winter months. Reservation only. Call 505-785-2232 ext. 429 for reservations, which require a VISA or MASTERCARD.
Special regulations:	No children under age 6. Must have bright flashlight with fresh batteries and good walking shoes. Photography permitted, but no tripods. Stay on cave trails at all times. Limited to 25 people.
Total distance:	1.25 miles in the cave plus 0.5 mile (one-way) to cave entrance and back.
Difficulty:	Moderate.
Time required:	2.5 hours in cave, plus 30-45 minutes to hike up to the cave entrance and 15-30 minutes to return to the trailhead.
Starting point:	Slaughter Canyon Trailhead.

Slaughter Canyon cave.

Finding the trailhead: To find the trailhead, take the paved road leading to Slaughter Canyon Cave which turns off U.S. Highway 62/180, 6 miles south of Whites City onto a well-marked paved road, County Road 418. The signs at the turnoff say "Slaughter Canyon Cave" and "Washington Ranch." Follow 418 for 10 miles until you reach the park boundary and the road turns to gravel. Follow the gravel road for another mile until it deadends at the trailhead. There is plenty of parking at the trailhead, which also has toilet and picnic facilities (no toilet facilities beyond this point).

The trail: Slaughter Canyon Cave is referred to as "New Cave" by many locals and in some old maps and guidebooks. However, the NPS has officially changed the name to Slaughter Canyon Cave. The canyon is named after Charles Slaughter who ranched there in the early 1900s.

The trail to the cave entrance is the first part of the experience. It's a well-used, well-constructed, well-defined trail—but it's steep! You climb more than 500 feet in a half mile. Since the trip actually starts at the cave entrance (not the trailhead in the parking lot) be sure to leave enough time to climb the hill to the cave so the ranger doesn't leave without you. The door to Slaughter Canyon Cave is always locked, so if you're late, you're out of luck.

This trip is not nearly as wild as others offered by the NPS. You can walk upright the entire way. It's a fairly easy trip with the exception of several slippery spots where the trail goes over ancient flowstone or polished bat guano. Without good-gripping shoes, you'll have a tough time in these sections.

56

Actually, you could call this "the guano walk." For most of the trip, you're walking on bat guano. There's no way to do the trip without stepping in it. Steps have been carved out in many places, but footing is still occasionally difficult.

Fortunately, the guano is about 28,000 years old, deposited by an extinct species of bat. It's reddish guano that has had all the nutrients leached out through the centuries. When discovered, there were no bats using the cave, and even now, no bats inhabit the cave, so no fresh guano. Miners took 50,000 tons of guano out of the cave, but all five companies that mined the cave went bankrupt because the nutrient-free guano made lousy fertilizer.

Like the natural entrance to Carlsbad Caverns, Slaughter Canyon Cave has a great "twilight zone," a short section where the natural light fades into total blackness.

Since the trip is popular with kids, rangers tell of the evil cave monster, The Hodag, known to frequent this cave, is an ugly brute with one red eye and only two legs—one short and one long for standing up straight on a cave wall.

Slaughter Canyon Cave has formations to equal anything in Carlsbad Caverns such as the Pillars of Hercules (just after Twilight Zone), Famous Clansman (filmed as part of the movie, King Solomon's Mine), and the fabulous Christmas Tree room. These are definitely among the most spectacular cave formations found anywhere.

Rangers talk frequently about how early miners destroyed parts of the cave before the NPS purchased it from them. At one spot in the cave, you view a pile of trash left by the miners. This spot now has the dubious distinction of being a federally protected junk pile.

6 LOWER CAVE

Type of trail:	Off-trail ranger-guided tour.
Schedule:	1 p.m. on Monday/Wednesday/Friday. Call ahead (1-505-785-2232 ext. 429) for reservations, which require a VISA or MASTERCARD.
Special regulations:	Bring your own batteries (four "AA" alkaline) and be sure you have good hiking boots or sturdy walking shoes. Stay on cave trails at all times. Limited to 12 people.
Total distance:	About 1 mile.
Difficulty:	Moderate.
Time required:	2.5 hours.
Starting point:	Visitor Center.

Finding the trailhead: To find the trailhead, turn west off U.S. Highway 62/180 at Whites City (20 miles south of Carlsbad, New Mexico) and drive 7 miles on a paved road to the park headquarters and visitor center.

The trail: The trip starts with a meeting at the top of the elevator in the visitor center. Ask at the front desk for directions.

After a brief orientation talk by the ranger and equipment check, you head down the elevator to the Big Room. You take the Big Room route for a short way before turning off and climbing down a series of ladders called "The Funnel." In this section, the going is difficult and slippery, as you descend 40 feet to Lower Cave.

Seldom-visited Lower Cave was featured by the National Geographic Magazine in the early 1900s. Lower Cave has lots of side passages, some of which have yet to be explored. Many research projects are underway in this, the deepest, section of Carlsbad Caverns.

After the Funnel, the route is fairly level. However, the trail is undeveloped. There's no nicely contoured, paved path like the Natural Entrance, Big Room, or King's Palace routes. You can walk normally all the way, so it also differs from the down-and-dirty Spider Cave and Hall of the White Giant routes.

Perhaps the highlight of the Lower cave route is the "Rookery." Here, the ranger points out "nests" of "cave pearls." The Rookery used to be carpeted with cave pearls, but there aren't many left. To illustrate how attitudes toward natural resource preservation have changed through the years, the early managers of the cave gathered up the cave pearls and gave one to each visitor as a souvenir. When you get to the "Jumping Off Point," the ceiling is high enough to clear a 25-story building with five feet to spare.

The Lower Cave route is a nice option for visitors who want more than the self-guided tours, but aren't ready to be amateur cavers.

7 SPIDER CAVE

Type of trail:	Off-trail ranger-guided tour plus a 1 mile hike to cave entrance.
Schedule:	1 p.m. on Sunday only. Call ahead (1-505-785-2232 ext. 429) for reservations, which require a VISA or MASTERCARD.
Special regulations:	Bring four "AA" alkaline batteries. Be sure you have good hiking boots or sturdy walking shoes, gloves and long pants. Limited to eight people. Old clothes are strongly recommended, as you're going to get dirty on this trip.
Total distance:	About 1 mile.
Difficulty:	Difficult.
Time required:	3-4 hours.
Starting point:	Visitor center.

Finding the trailhead: To find the trailhead, turn west off U.S. Highway 62\180 at Whites City (20 miles south of Carlsbad, New Mexico) and drive 7 miles on a paved road to the park headquarters and visitor center.

The trail: At the visitor center, the rangers equip you with lights, knee and elbow pads, and give a short orientation talk. Then, the group drives their own vehicles about 1 mile to the parking area at the beginning of Scenic Loop Drive. From the parking area, you hike about 0.5 mile into nearby Garden Grove Canyon, down a steep descent to the dry wash and the entrance to Spider Cave. This is a difficult, but short, hike.

Checking damage to formations in Spider Cave. NPS photo.

Experienced cavers love Spider Cave, but it can be intimidating for the novice. Even the name is intimidating and, yes, the cave was named for hordes of spiders (actually daddy longlegs, which are not arachnids, so technically, are not spiders) found clinging to the ceiling when first discovered—but they're gone now.

Then after you get past the arachnophobia, it gets worse. The entrance to the cave has been built up out of the arroyo like the opening to a manhole. As the ranger unlocks the "manhole cover," it's easy to wonder what the NPS has locked up down there.

You then climb down a ladder and crawl through a narrow, muddy passage for 50 yards or so. Hopefully, your arachnophobia doesn't turn to claustrophobia because you can't go back. It's too tight to turn around.

The group stops for a rest in the first big chamber. This doesn't happen on the guided tour, but if the ranger decided to have the blackout early and be really quiet at this point, inexperienced cavers might hear the real sounds of a narrow cave passage—adrenaline flowing and hearts pounding.

Although the initial rush might test your courage, the trip soon turns into a fantastic experience. You're not likely to forget your trip to Spider Cave. In fact, if the NPS wanted to convert park visitors into cavers, the trip to Spider Cave would be a great introduction.

If you've already been in the Big Room, you'll notice the stark contrast with Spider Cave. Everything seems to be miniature in comparison—some of the same type of speleothems, but they are 6 feet instead of 60 feet tall, and equally beautiful. Most of the rock and dirt in Spider Cave is a reddish color, which contrasts sharply with many splendid white formations.

Spider Cave has about 3 miles of explored passages, but this trip is less than a mile long. Even though the cave is near Carlsbad Caverns, there is no known connection.

On this trip, like many others, rangers spend time discussing cave preservation by showing how early explorers have destroyed precious formations. Once despoiled, cave features are extremely difficult or impossible to reclaim and, of course, it would take several million years to grow them again.

8 HALL OF THE WHITE GIANT

Type of trail:	Off-trail ranger-guided tour.
Schedule:	1 p.m. on Saturday only. Call ahead (1-505-785-2232 ext. 429) for reservations, which require a VISA or MASTERCARD.
Special regulations:	Bring four "AA" alkaline batteries. Be sure you have good hiking boots or sturdy walking shoes, gloves, and long pants. Limited to 10 people.
Total distance:	About 0.5 mile.
Time required:	3-4 hours.
Difficulty:	Difficult.
Starting point:	Visitor center.

Finding the trailhead: To find the trailhead, turn west off U.S. Highway 62/180 at Whites City (20 miles south of Carlsbad, New Mexico) and drive 7 miles on a paved road to the park headquarters and visitor center.

The trail: This trip, like Spider Cave, adds a whole new dimension to a visit to Carlsbad Caverns. This is one of the "wild caving experiences" the NPS mentions in its literature.

After getting equipped with hard-hats, head lamps, knee and elbow pads, and hearing a brief introduction by the ranger, you head out of the visitor center on the

Signing the register at the end of the trip to Hall of the White Giant.

Natural Entrance route. About halfway down, the ranger stops and directs you to a small passage, which—compared to the huge cavern you're standing in—doesn't even look like a cave. In fact, if you've walked down the manicured path from the Natural Entrance on an earlier trip, you obviously walked right past the entrance to the passage leading to the Hall of the White Giant without even noticing it.

It's only a half mile, but it takes more than three hours. Along the way you'll use (or quickly learn) some beginning rock climbing skills like chimneying. You also climb up and down well-placed ladders, over slippery flowstone, and through some incredibly tight spots to reach your goal—the Hall of the White Giant.

The White Giant might not be as spectacular as the giant formations in the Big Room, King's Palace, or Slaughter Canyon Cave, but all the work you have to do to see it might make the White Giant the most spectacular of them all. When you get there, you'll take turns using a rope to climb over slick flowstone to get a closer view of the magnificent formation. Then, after everybody has had a turn, the ranger does the traditional "blackout" where everybody remains totally quiet with only the sounds of the caves permeating the utter blackness. This gives you the stark essence of the cave.

GUADALUPE MOUNTAINS NATIONAL PARK

OVERVIEW MAP

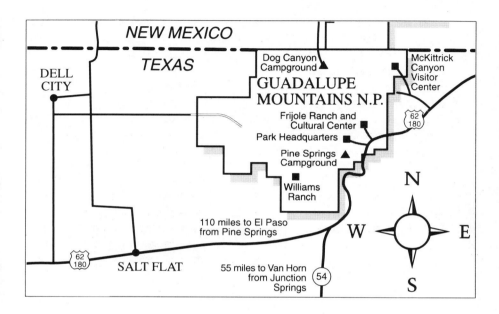

OVERVIEW

Named after the patron saint of Mexico, the Guadalupe Mountains highlight the horizon of west Texas. The mountain range contains the four tallest peaks in Texas and what has frequently been called "the best view in Texas," the vista from the top of Hunter Peak. Another section of the park, McKittrick Canyon, has been labeled "the most beautiful spot in Texas."

In these mountains, which loom 3,700 feet above the salt flats of northwestern Texas, the plants and animals of the desert meet those of the mountains, as do the southern species meet the northern species. They all make a home, together and symbolically, here in the Guadalupes.

The 86,416-acre park provides a fragile environment for 58 mammals, 260 birds, and hundreds of distinct plant species. "The National Park Highway" (U.S. Highway 62/180) provides tantalizing glimpses of the beauty beyond, especially the protruding landmark El Capitan, visible for 50 miles in any direction. Three major trailheads provide access to the backcountry, and more than 80 miles of trails offer scenic avenues for the human species to see it all.

The Pine Springs Trailhead leads to most of the park's trails, and it has a campground, picnic area, and visitor center (open 8 a.m. to 6 p.m. MST, Memorial Day to Labor Day, and 8 a.m. to 4:30 p.m. MST in winter months). McKittrick Canyon

Trailhead offers an easy and popular trail through the incredible beauty and diversity of that hidden canyon. But at an elevation of 6,300 feet, the secluded Dog Canyon Trailhead offers the easiest route to the heart of the Guadalupes.

Guadalupe Mountains National Park is a haven for both geologists and botanists. Even visitors totally unfamiliar and uninterested in geology and botany routinely leave the park as amateur botanists and geologists.

The trail system is very well constructed, maintained, and organized. The National Park Service has worked hard to provide great trails, and the extra effort really shows. The trail system offers the variety and convenience many hikers prefer. This book outlines the most popular routes, but the trail system allows the creative hiker to craft his or her own adventures. Only the Blue Ridge Trail and Marcus Trail in the far northwestern corner of the park are less-than-ideal trails.

To fully enjoy the Guadalupes, however, hikers must be in a proper frame of mind.

First, get water out of your mind. The Guadalupes have no reliable water sources. Although your pack can grow heavy with the weight of water, you'll soon realize that a landscape does not need a mountain lake or waterfall to be scenic.

Second, the wind can really blow, especially in the spring. And this isn't a wimpy wind like you find in Chicago. This is a real, Herculean wind, often gusting to more than 50 mph and as fast as 125 mph. It's weird, too. It comes up suddenly, blows you off the trail, and then goes away, only to return when you least expect it. You can be walking along, leaning into the wind at a 45-degree angle, and then, just like that, it stops blowing and you fall down. Instead of looking at the wind as a problem, look at it as a special feature and challenge of the Guadalupes.

Entrance sign with El Capitan in background. NPS photo by D. Allen.

You can hike year-round in the Guadalupes, but the summer heat can be miserable, and snow can blanket the high country during winter months. The "shoulder seasons"—March/April/May and September/October/November—usually offer the best hiking weather.

GETTING TO GUADALUPE MOUNTAINS NATIONAL PARK

From El Paso, Texas, drive east 102 miles on U.S. Highway 62/180 to Pine Springs, the location of the park headquarters and visitor center. From Carlsbad, New Mexico, drive south 40 miles on U.S. Highway 62/180 into Texas to Pine Springs. If you're flying in and renting a car, it's best to use the El Paso airport. Keep in mind that there are no services within 30 miles of the park, so arrive there with a full tank of gas and all the supplies you need for your stay.

PINE SPRINGS TRAILHEAD

The Pine Springs area serves as the park headquarters. It has a large visitor center, the park's largest campground, and a sizable picnic area. The trailhead is located at the far end of the campground. There's plenty of parking, and hikers can get backcountry camping permits at the nearby visitor center.

This is a major trailhead. Trails go in all directions, and in fact, the majority of the park's trails can be reached from here.

The Pine Springs area also has a rich and colorful history. The Old Butterfield Stage Route passed through here; the ruins of stagecoach station, The Pinery, lies near the visitor center. The U.S. Army used the area before the Civil War and after the campaign against the Mescalero Apache.

The main reason for all the early activity was a reliable water source at Lower Pine Springs. However, the spring dried up after a 1931 earthquake.

FIND THE TRAILHEAD

Turn off of U.S. Highway 62/180 at the main entrance of Guadalupe Mountains National Park. Immediately take a left turn into the campground. Drive to the far end of the campground to the well-marked trailhead. The trailhead has toilet facilities and a large parking lot. If the lot is full, you can also park in the visitor center parking lot and use a short connecting trail to get from the visitor center to the trailhead. Don't park in the marked campsites in the nearby campground.

Also included under the Pine Springs Trailhead section of this book are trails leaving the Williams Ranch and the Frijole Ranch. Please refer to these trails for specific directions to these trailheads.

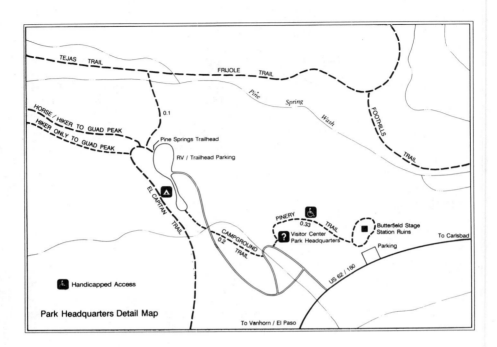

Park Headquarters Detail Map

1 THE PINERY

Type of Trail:	Out and back, shuttle, or loop.
Type of trip:	Self-guided day hike.
Total distance:	0.75 mile.
Difficulty:	Easy, accessible to people with mobility impairments.
Elevation change:	Minimal
Time required:	Less than one hour.
Maps:	Free park brochure available at visitor center.
Starting point:	Pine Springs Visitor Center or from a turnoff from U.S. Highway 62/180 just 1 mile north of the park headquarters.

The trail: For a brief introduction to the low-elevation environment of Guadalupe Mountains National Park, take this short nature trail from the visitor center to The Pinery. The trail starts right at the front door of the Pine Springs Visitor Center.

The trail gets its name from an old stagecoach horse changing station located on the Butterfield Trail, a 2,800-mile overland mail route in 1800s. The station, located on 5,534-foot Guadalupe Pass, was named for the stands of pine nearby. Today, U.S. Highway 62/180 generally follows the stage route through Guadalupe Pass.

The Pinery Trail is a paved, self-guided tour with excellent interpretive signs covering the history of the area and offering tantalizing details on several plant species in the area. You travel about a 0.25 mile from the visitors center to the ruins of the station, then around the ruins and back to the visitor center. You can also have somebody pick you up at the parking lot on U.S. Highway 62/180 just north of the turn-off to Pine springs.

2 SALT BASIN OVERLOOK

Type of Trail:	Loop (actually a "lollipop") with an out-and-back section.
Type of trip:	Long day hike.
Total distance:	11.5 miles.
Difficulty:	Moderate.
Elevation change:	500 feet.
Time required:	6-8 hours.
Maps:	Trails Illustrated Guadalupe Mountains Map and USGS Guadalupe Peak and Guadalupe Pass, and the free park brochure.
Starting point:	Pine Springs Trailhead.

Key points:

0.05 Junction with Guadalupe Peak and Frijole Trails.
3.4 Guadalupe Canyon and junction with loop trail.
4.3 Second junction with loop trail.
7.9 Junction with main trail at Guadalupe Canyon.
11.5 Pine Springs Trailhead.

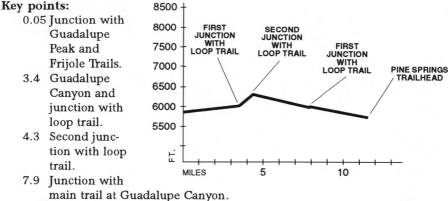

The trail: For those who want a long day hike without much climbing, the Salt Basin Overlook Trail is an excellent choice. Set aside a entire day for this trip, which leaves an hour or two for relaxing along the way. The trail is well-defined all the way with the exception of one short stretch where it dips into Guadalupe Canyon on the lower loop.

About 100 feet after leaving the campground, the trail forks and then forks again in another 100 feet. Take the left fork at both junctions.

The trail gradually climbs (460 feet in about 3 miles) toward El Capitan before dropping into beautiful Guadalupe Canyon, where you'll find the junction with the Salt Basin Loop Trail. You'll start getting good looks at El Capitan after about 1.5 miles. If you're taking the loop, it's easier to continue on straight (southwest) on the

Salt Basin Overlook
El Capitan • Guadalupe Peak

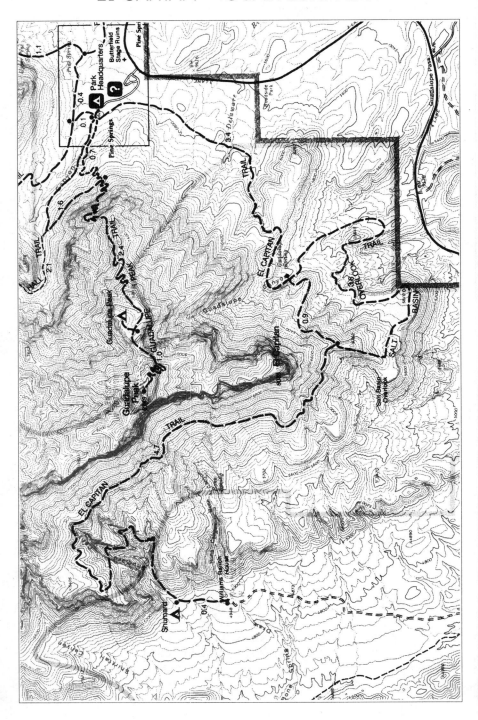

El Capitan trail for 0.9 mile to the second junction, and then take the loop counterclockwise.

The views from the El Capitan Trail equal those from any place on the loop, so if you're interested in a 8.6-mile hike instead of a 11.5-mile hike, you can make this an out-and-back hike by retracing your steps back to the campground from the second junction and call it a good day. The loop adds 3.6 miles of new terrain to the trip, but from a scenery standpoint, it doesn't add much.

If you take the loop, the trail drops sharply from the second junction (a good reason to do the loop counterclockwise) down to the ruins of an old water tank. Along this half-mile stretch you get great views into the salt flats to the southwest. Be sure to look back a few times to view the stately El Capitan looming over you to the north. At about the 3-mile mark on the loop, the trail drops down into an arroyo for about 0.25 mile, but cairns lead the way.

The wind often whips through this area, especially in the spring and especially around the second junction, so hang onto your hat. Just when it starts to seem like you've been trapped in a hair drier for life, the wind suddenly stops blowing.

Also, there is virtually no shade along this route, so be prepared for a full day in the sun.

3 EL CAPITAN

Type of trail: Shuttle.
Type of trip: Long day hike.
Total distance: 9.4 miles.
Difficulty: Moderate.
Elevation change: 1,530 feet.
Time required: 6-9 hours, plus driving time to Williams Ranch.
Maps: Trails Illustrated Guadalupe Mountains Map and USGS PX Flat and Guadalupe Peak and the free park brochure.
Starting point: Williams Ranch.

Key points:
0.4 Shumard Camp.
4.6 El Capitan
5.1 First junction with lower loop.
6.0 Second junction with lower loop.
9.4 Pine Springs Trailhead.

Finding the trailhead: The first step in getting to the trailhead is a visit to the visitor center where you ask for a key to the gates on the way to the Williams Ranch. This is a four-wheel-drive road—definitely not for low-clearance vehicles. Park regulations prohibit leaving vehicles at the trailhead.

To find the trailhead, drive south on U.S. Highway 62/180 from the main entrance to Guadalupe Mountains National Park for 8 miles and turn right (west). Be alert,

The trail up Shumard Canyon.

as this turn is poorly marked with no sign except a National Park Service shield on the brown gate. Use the key to unlock the gate and then be sure to lock it behind you; and ditto for a second gate about a mile up the road. The NPS has arranged public access across this mile-long strip of private land paralleling the highway, but remember this is private land, so be sure to stay on the road.

Beyond the second gate, you're in the park. Slowly bump and grind up the road, which gets rough in places, until it ends at the Williams Ranch Trailhead. It takes about an hour to get to Williams Ranch from the visitor center.

The trail: This is definitely one of the most spectacular hikes in the Guadalupe Mountains. Unfortunately, it requires some special effort to arrange a shuttle to Williams Ranch. When you get out on the trail, however, you'll consider the extra hassle worth it compared to the effort involved in making this an 18.8-mile, out-and-back hike from Pine Springs.

You could consider getting to the trailhead as part of the experience. The primitive road to the trailhead generally follows parts of the Butterfield Stagecoach Trail used in the mid-1800s. The Williams Ranch was a working ranching operation in the early 1900s where Robert Belcher ran longhorn cattle. Later, Uncle Dalph Williams ran cattle, sheep, and goats there until 1942. The NPS has preserved the historic ranch house at the trailhead. On the way to Williams Ranch you can see the aftermath of overgrazing in this dry climate, as the original grassland has been replaced by an ocean of greasewood.

This is the only trail into the remote western portion of the Guadalupe Mountains. Don't plan on seeing many people (at least until you get to the Guadalupe Canyon area), because this area receives much less use than most other trails in the park. Starting from the west end at Williams Ranch allows you to end at the Pine Springs Campground and have the often strong westerly winds at your back most of the way.

From the trailhead, the trail climbs up Shumard Canyon. The grade doesn't seem steep, but it's a healthy climb, gaining over 1,300 feet in the first 2 miles. The scenery is spectacular, which may be one reason the climb doesn't seem as precipitous as it is. At several points while climbing up the canyon, you get great views down the canyon and out into the flats to the west. Ahead you can see Shumard Peak and the great escarpment of the Guadalupe Mountains.

About 0.5 mile from the trailhead, you'll find the designated Shumard campsite. It's well-signed and about 100 yards off to the left (west) with five tent sites all flattened and rock-free, thanks to the NPS.

Beyond the head of Shumard Canyon, the trail turns south and levels out and passes the head of sprawling Bone Canyon. For the next 3 miles, you hike in the shadow of the Guadalupe escarpment, gradually gaining another 200 feet. You essentially walk around El Capitan, the venerable symbol of Guadalupe Mountains National Park. You can look down and see the cars traveling the highway below, but you have a much better view than these travelers do.

After 5.1 miles, you reach the first junction with the Salt Basin Overlook loop trail. If you want to stretch the hike out for an additional 3.6 miles, take the lower loop trail. However, this lower loop adds little more than distance to the trip. The scenery from above at least equals anything you see on the lower loop.

After another 0.9 mile, you drop down into Guadalupe Canyon where you find the other end of the lower loop trail. From here, it's 3.4 miles to the Pine Springs trailhead, all fairly level and easy walking.

Williams Ranch at the Shumard Canyon Trailhead.

The El Capitan Trail is better suited for a long day hike than an overnighter. The Shumard campsite is located at the beginning (or the end) of the trail, which means you would hike the entire trail in one day whether you do an overnighter or a day hike. However, for the well-conditioned hiker, this can be a nice overnight, out-and-back trip from the Pine Springs Trailhead if you don't have somebody to give you a ride around to the Williams Ranch.

This trail is well-defined and easy to follow the entire way. Just before you reach the Pine Springs Trailhead, the trail forks twice. Take the right fork at both junctions.

4   GUADALUPE PEAK

Type of trail: Out and back.
Type of trip: Day hike or overnighter.
Total distance: 8.4 miles.
Difficulty: Difficult.
Elevation change: 2,930 feet.
Time required: 6-8 hours.
Maps: Trails Illustrated Guadalupe Mountains Map and USGS Guadalupe Peak and the park brochure.
Starting point: Pine Springs Campground.

See Map on Page 68

Key points:
0.05 Junction with Frijole and El Capitan Trails.
0.1 Junction with Guadalupe Peak horse trail.
0.8 Second junction with Guadalupe Peak horse trail.
3.2 Guadalupe Peak Camp.
4.2 Guadalupe Peak.
8.4 Pine Springs Trailhead.

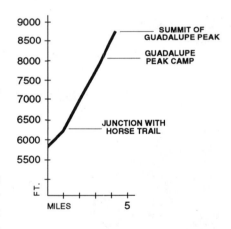

The trail: For more than one reason, this trail is the high point of Guadalupe Mountains National Park. Guadalupe Peak is not only the highest spot in the park, but also in all of Texas. At 8,749 feet, Guadalupe Peak might pale in comparison to the 14,000-foot summits of California and Colorado, but in terms of relief, elevation gain, and sheer beauty, it can be compared with any mountain in the lower 48 states.

Besides being the highest elevation, the trip to Guadalupe Peak is bound to be the "high point" of any visit to the park. In fact, this is one of the most spectacular hikes in the United States. If you only have one day to hike in the Guadalupe Mountains and you're of average or better fitness level, this hike should be top priority.

If possible, start early. This hike climbs nearly 3,000 feet, so you want to take advantage of the cooler temperatures of the early morning. Take plenty of water.

The trail climbs the entire 4.2 miles to the highest point in Texas, but fortunately, the trail has been expertly constructed to minimize the damage to your legs and lungs.

Nonetheless, it's a tough hike, so get ready to put out some sweat to reach the summit. You shouldn't try this hike unless you are in at least average physical condition. This trail will certainly dispel lingering myths about Texas being flat.

The NPS allows horses on this trail to within a 100 yards of the summit, but horse use is limited, as the serious elevation gain with no water sources makes this trail too difficult for many horses. Backcountry horsemen take the longer route (see map) instead of the steeper 0.7-mile segment reserved for hikers only.

After about 2 miles, you might think you see the top and might start thinking you were in better shape than you thought. But beware, this is a false summit; you're only about halfway there. You might want to occupy your mind studying the major shift in biomes—from desert vegetation like cactus and yucca to the higher-elevation pine forests.

A mile before the summit, watch for a sign for the campground, which lies on a rare level spot on the mountain about 200 yards to the right of the main trail. This is the highest campground in Texas, and it's so special that it's probably worth the 2,000-foot climb with a heavy pack to get there. There are five flattened, rock-free tent sites with spectacular views. It would be hard to beat the amenities of this campground. If you decide to camp overnight, stake your tent well, as the wind can be vicious on Guadalupe Peak, especially in the spring.

At the summit, you obviously get the grandest view possible. Bush Mountain (8,631 feet) and Shumard Peak (8,615 feet) to the north are the second and third highest peaks in Texas. To the south stretches the vast flatness of the Chihauhuan Desert, broken only by the Delaware and Sierra Diablos mountains. On a clear day, you can see the 12,003-foot Sierra Blanca, more than 100 miles to the north.

Guadalupe Peak and El Capitan viewed from the ridge above Pine Springs Canyon.

The top of El Capitan from the Guadalupe Peak Trail.

After taking in the vistas all around, you might want to write some stirring personal impressions in the trail register at the top. In 1958, American Airlines placed a pyramid-shaped monument on the summit to commemorate the 100th anniversary of transcontinental mail delivery, which went through Guadalupe Pass.

On the way down, you can see Pine Springs Campground and say "I climbed up here!" You also get a great view of Hunter Peak (8,368 feet) and the massive Pine Springs Canyon. You can also see the Tejas Trail angling up the south side of Hunter Peak.

When you finally reach the campground, you can relax for awhile and relish in the thought that you will leave the Guadalupe Mountains with the life-long memory of a truly unforgettable hike.

5   DEVIL'S HALL

Type of trail: Out and back.
Type of trip: Day hike.
Total distance: 4.2 miles.
Difficulty: Moderate.
Elevation change: 400 feet.
Time required: 3-5 hours.
Maps: Trails Illustrated Guadalupe Mountains Map and USGS Guadalupe Peak and the park brochure.
Starting point: Pine Springs Campground.

Devil's Hall. NPS photo by D. Allen.

Key points:

0.05 Junction with the Tejas and Guadalupe
   Peak Trails.
1.0 Junction with Devil's Hall Trail.
2.1 Devil's Hall.
4.2 Pine Springs Trailhead.

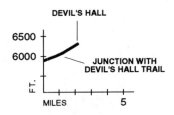

The trail: The first mile of this trip follows a well-
defined trail up Pine Springs Canyon. This is the horse route up Guadalupe Peak,
so the trail is well-defined and easy to follow.

The trail passes through the scars left by the man-caused, 6,510-acre Pine Fire
of 1993. This is a stark reminder to be careful with fire in this dry, fragile environment. Note that this fire, like most wildland fires, did not burn everything. Instead,
wildfire tends to leave some plants unburnt, which helps re-vegetate the area.

At the end of the first mile, the main trail switchbacks to the left toward the
Guadalupe Peak Trail. At this switchback, you'll notice a sign indicating that the trail
continues along the canyon wash. Go straight on the less-developed trail.

For the first 100 yards after the sign, the trail is rocky and rough, and then it
disappears completely. You spend most of the rest of the trip walking up the canyon wash. It's another mile to Devil's Hall.

The walking gets rough here and there, so pick your way carefully. Watch for small
and infrequent cairns, but don't panic if you can't see one. You won't get lost as long
as you stay in the streambed.

Just before Devil's Hall, the canyon narrows at a spot sometimes called Devil's
Gate. Shortly thereafter, you go up a stair-step-like series of ledges called the Hiker's
Staircase. Then, you can see where the canyon has been pinched down to about 15
feet at Devil's Hall.

Devil's Hall is an unusual spot where the streambed narrows and slips between
two pillars of rock. Much of the rock in the area looks like it was laid down like fine
masonry.

Although the rock formations seem to be the focal point of this trip, they might
not be the most scenic part of the hike. That distinction might go to the diverse and
colorful vegetation in the area. The entire hike goes through the desert riparian zone,
but the last mile follows a narrow canyon where the shade provided by canyon walls
and the extra vegetation of the streambed has created a showcase of dryland flora.
The canyon is lined with velvet ash, Texas madrone, bigtooth maple, ponderosa pine
and many other tree species. In the fall, it can be almost as colorful as McKittrick
Canyon, but with fewer people.

For beginning hikers, this hike provides an opportunity to gain confidence by
getting off trail—and surviving.

The NPS advises against going any farther up the canyon than Devil's Hall, and
a sign marks the end of the trail. After taking a good break, retrace your steps to the
campground. If you have the time and energy, you can take a different route back,
by taking a right when you hit the main trail again and after 0.6 mile, taking another
left down the Guadalupe Peak Trail to the campground.

One note of caution. Avoid this hike on afternoons when thunderstorms are likely.
You would not want to be caught at Devil's Hall in a flash flood.

DEVIL'S HALL • HUNTER PEAK • THE BOWL
SMITH SPRING • FOOTHILLS

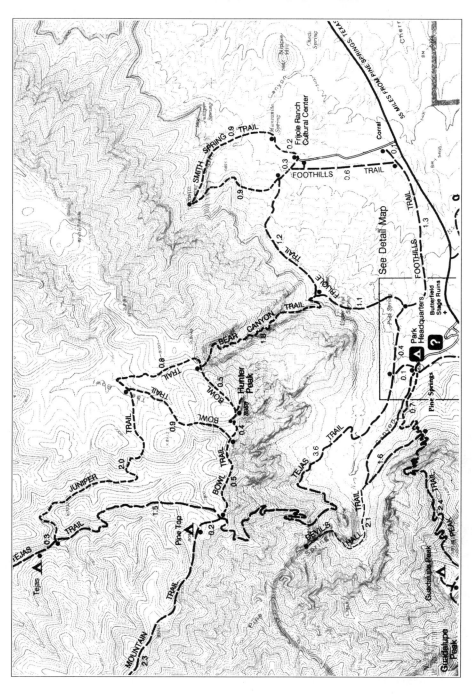

6 HUNTER PEAK

Type of trail: Loop.
Type of trip: Day hike or overnighter.
Total distance: 8.5 miles.
Difficulty: Difficult.
Elevation change: 2,546 feet, if you go to top of Hunter Peak.
Time required: 6-8 hours.
Maps: Trails Illustrated Guadalupe Mountains Map and USGS Guadalupe Peak and the park brochure.
Starting point: Pine Springs Campground

See Map on Page 77

Key points:

0.05 El Capitan/Guadalupe Peak Trail Junction.
0.1 Tejas Trail Junction.
3.7 Bush Mountain Trail Junction.
4.2 The Bowl Trail Junction.
4.6 Spur trail to summit of Hunter Peak.
5.1 Bear Canyon Trail Junction.
6.9 Frijole Trail Junction.
8.0 Foothills Trail Junction.
8.4 Tejas Trail Junction.
8.5 Pine Springs Trailhead.

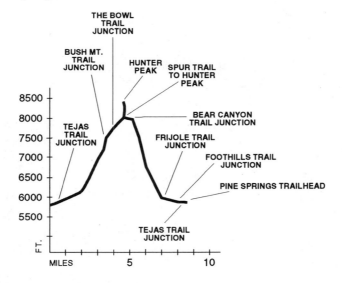

The trail: When considering this hike, one big question comes up right away—clockwise or counterclockwise? This question is often debated among local hikers and park rangers with, unfortunately, no consensus. It really comes down to personal preference. Do you prefer to gain elevation fast and get it behind you as quickly as possible? Or do you like a long, gradual climb without as many steep grades? Counterclockwise is easier on knees, but clockwise is easier on lungs.

If you're in the "get it over with" camp, go counterclockwise, up Bear Canyon and down the Tejas Trail (3.9 miles to the high point just below Hunter Peak, with most elevation gained in a 1.8-mile stretch up Bear Canyon). If you like a longer, more gradual climb, go clockwise, up the Tejas Trail and down Bear Canyon (4.8 miles to the same high point, with a moderate grade most of the way.) This trail description is written for the clockwise route.

Immediately after leaving Pine Springs Campground, you take a right at a major junction, with trails going off to the left to Guadalupe Peak and El Capitan and straight to Devil's Hall. You go right on the Frijole Trail. Then, in another 200 yards or so, after crossing the expansive dry wash of Pine Springs Canyon, you hit another junction with the Frijole Trail going straight. Turn left and head north up the hill on the Tejas Trail. You'll be coming back down the Frijole Trail.

The next mile is nearly flat with an almost imperceptible increase in elevation. Then, you start a moderate climb up to Pine Top, about 2,000 vertical feet over 3 miles of well-designed trail that minimizes the impact of the elevation gain. This trail is as good as a trail can be, but it still doesn't make this an easy hike, especially on a hot day with an overnight pack. Plan on 2 to 3 hours to get to Pine Top—and longer if you have a heavy pack.

Like many spots in the Guadalupe Mountains, especially in the spring, the wind can whip through Pine Springs Canyon. You can try to forget the wind by watching the vegetation gradually change switchback after switchback, and then dramatically change the instant you crest the edge of the escarpment and enter the high-altitude forest of ponderosa pine, limber pine and Douglas-fir.

If you're staying overnight, you must have a permit for the Pine Top Campground, which is 0.2 mile to your left when you enter the forest. The campground has six

Old Butterfied Stage Station with Hunter Peak in the background. NPS photo by F. Many.

View of Pine Springs area from the top of Bear Canyon.

tent sites all leveled and squared, courtesy of the NPS. This campground has a better view than many other campsites in the park. To finish the loop, you'll have to retrace that 0.2 mile the next morning.

If you're day hiking, take a right at the junction at the top of the escarpment (the 4.2-mile mark) and head east on the Bowl Trail toward Hunter Peak. After a long half mile, the Bowl Trail splits, and you take the righthand fork, staying on the rim of the escarpment.

Shortly after the split, you'll see a spur trail heading off to the right and climbing up to 8,368-foot Hunter Peak. This junction is the high point of the main trail, but it's another 150 vertical feet or so to the top of Hunter Peak on the spur trail. If you're backpacking, shed your pack here and take the 0.25-mile climb up to the top of Hunter Peak for a rest break and a great view of Guadalupe Peak and El Capitan and of the entire Pine Springs and Frijole area—plus, it seems, all of Texas. It looks like you're level with Guadalupe Peak, but Hunter Peak is 381 feet lower.

After dropping down to the main trail, you finally start going downhill. In less than a half mile, you'll see the junction with the Bear Canyon Trail. You'll also be able to see how steep the narrow canyon is compared with the longer switchbacks up the Tejas Trail. You might also wonder how (and why!) ranchers in the early 1900s pumped water for livestock all the way up Bear Canyon. Some hikers might find this stretch of trail too steep to comfortably hike without slipping or feeling some pain in their knees, but it's short, only 1.8 miles to the junction with the Frijole Trail.

By the time you reach the Frijole Trail, you've seen a rapid change in the vegetation, going from the pine forest, through riparian vegetation like bigtooth maple and then out into the yucca and prickly pear of the desert, all in less than 2 miles.

Take a right at the Frijole Trail Junction and continue to descend, albeit more gradually, toward Pine Springs. After 1.1 miles, you hit the Foothills Trail where you take a right and continue on the Frijole Trail as it heads west another 1.8 miles to the trailhead, passing through the two junctions you saw at the beginning of your hike. The last 1.8 miles is, believe it or not, flat.

7 THE BOWL

Type of trail: Loop.
Type of trip: Primarily an overnighter, but could be done as a long day hike.

See Map on Page 77

Total distance: 13 miles with an overnight stay at the Tejas Campsite.
Difficulty: Difficult.
Elevation change: 2,546 feet, if you go to the top of Hunter Peak.
Time required: 6-9 hours.
Maps: Trails Illustrated Guadalupe Mountains Map and USGS Guadalupe Peak and the park brochure.
Starting point: Pine Springs Campground.

Key points:
0.05 El Capitan/Guadalupe Peak Trail Junction.
0.1 Tejas Trail Junction.
3.7 Bush Mountain Trail Junction.
5.2 Junction with Juniper Trail.
5.5 Tejas Camp.
5.8 Junction with Juniper Trail.
7.8 Junction with Bowl Trail.
8.7 Junction with Hunter Peak Trail.
9.1 Spur trail to summit of Hunter Peak.
9.6 Bear Canyon Trail Junction.
11.4 Frijole Trail Junction.
12.5 Foothills Trail Junction.
12.9 Tejas Trail Junction.
13.0 Pine Springs Trailhead.

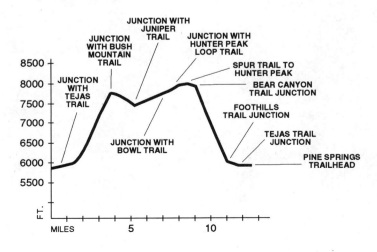

The trail: This trip is, in essence, an elongated overnight version of hike number 6, the Hunter Peak Loop. Like the Hunter Peak Loop, this route is described in a clockwise manner. For details on the first part of the trip, from Pine Springs Campground to Pine Top, refer to the Hunter Peak Loop trail description.

If you're staying overnight, you must choose your campsite before leaving and get the required backcountry permit from the Pine Springs Visitor Center. The first preference might be the Tejas Campsite, which is as close as you can get to the midpoint of the trip. However, you can also stay at Pine Top, which is 0.2 mile to your left once you reach the rim of the escarpment. If you plan on a late start on the first day and don't mind a long second day, you might prefer Pine Top.

At the top of the big climb up from Pine Springs, you hit a crossroads-type junction where you can go all four directions. Go straight (north) staying on the Tejas Trail. The next 1.5 miles pass through the beautiful relict forest of the Guadalupe high country. You drop down about 300 feet in elevation along the way.

The Tejas Campsite is 0.3 mile past the Juniper Trail junction on the left (west) side of the trail. It has four tent sites. From tent site number 1, you get a good view of an old water tank, part of the historic water system used by ranchers to facilitate livestock grazing in the Bowl.

The next morning, you retrace the 0.3 mile on the Tejas Trail to the Juniper Trail junction and take a left onto the Juniper Trail. Like the section of the Tejas Trail, the Juniper Trail is just a wonderful walk in the woods. The trail is in great shape, and

The narrow and steep Bear Canyon Trail.

Old water tanks along the Bowl Trail.

nature improves it with a carpet of pine needles and oak leaves. It has junipers, of course, but seemingly no more than many other trails in the Guadalupe high country.

Watch carefully for elk, the monarch of the Guadalupe Mountains, as the oversized ungulates frequently hang out in this neck of the woods. In September and October, you can often hear the drawn-out bugle of the bull elk as you hike through the deep forest of the Bowl.

Along the Juniper Trail, you'll see frequent signs of the ancient water delivery system—several old water tanks and a pipe running along the trail. Instead of looking at the rusting pipes and tanks as eyesores on the unspoiled face of the wilderness, consider them lingering reminders of why we need national parks.

After 2 miles on the Juniper Trail, you hit a junction with the Bowl Trail. This forces a tough decision. You can complete the loop by going either left or right. Both trails go to the Bear Canyon Trail Junction. Both trails continue to pass through the relict forest, with the Juniper Trail passing through a more open forest heavy with deciduous trees.

If you've already seen the view from Hunter Peak, you might try the left fork, which stays on the Juniper Trail for 0.8 mile before hitting the Bear Canyon Trail junction. This cuts 1 mile of your trip, unless you drop your pack at the Bear Canyon Trail Junction and take a 1-mile side trip up to the top of Hunter Peak and back.

If you haven't seen what has been called the "best view in Texas" from the top of Hunter Peak, you might want to take the longer route down the Bowl Trail. After a pleasant 0.9 mile, this trail hits the Bowl Trail, 0.4 mile from the short spur trail up to Hunter Peak, where you simply must drop your pack and take this 0.25-mile hike to the summit. After soaking in the view, go back to the Bowl Trail and take a right (east) and follow the Bowl Trail along the rim of the escarpment for another 0.5 mile to the Bear Canyon Trail Junction.

Take the Bear Canyon Trail down to the Frijole Trail and back to Pine Springs Campground. Refer to the Hunter Peak Loop trail for more details on the rest of the loop.

8 SMITH SPRING

See Map on Page 77

Type of trail: Loop
Type of trip: Day hike.
Total distance: 2.3 miles.
Difficulty: Easy to moderate.
Elevation change: 440 feet.
Time required: 1.5-2.5 hours.
Maps: Trails Illustrated Guadalupe Mountains Map and USGS Guadalupe Peak and park brochure.
Starting point: Frijole Ranch.

Key points:
0.2 Manzanita Spring.
1.1 Smith Spring.
2.0 Junction with Frijole Trail.
2.2 Junction with Foothills Trail.
2.3 Frijole Ranch.

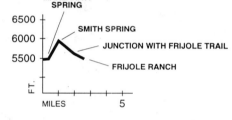

Finding the trailhead: Drive north from the main entrance to Guadalupe Mountains National Park on U.S. Highway 62/180 for 1 mile and turn (left) north. The turn-off is well-signed as "Frijole Ranch." Head up the well-maintained gravel road for about 0.5 mile until it deadends at the historic ranch and museum.

The trail: For somebody who wants a short, easy hike that really captures the essence and diversity of the desert environment, the Smith Spring loop is ideal. It's only 2.3 miles with slight elevation gain, and it goes to lush and beautiful Smith Spring, which probably comes closer to fitting the stereotypical image of a desert oasis than any other place in the Guadalupe Mountains.

You can hike the loop either way, of course, but the counterclockwise is described here. This route allows you to start out on the easiest section of the trail and visit Manzanita Springs only 0.2 mile after leaving the trailhead. To take the counterclockwise route, do not take the trail just on the left of the sign at the trailhead. Instead take the trail at the north edge of the ranch and museum.

The trail to Manzanita Spring is accessible to people with mobility impairments, and it's very easy walking. Watch for elk, deer, and other wildlife on this trip. The wild residents of the Guadalupe Mountains use the springs to quench their desert thirst. Try to plan the trip for evening to increase your chances of seeing wildlife.

Manzanita Spring is a marshy pond that's used heavily by wildlife as a water source, witnessed by the omnipresent animal tracks around the spring. This is also the site of a horrific attack on the Mescalero Apache where Lt. Howard Cushing

Manzanita Springs with Nipple Hill in the background.

destroyed a large winter cache of food, which probably resulted in the winter starvation of tribal members who managed to escape the raid. A lengthy interpretive sign at Manzanita Spring gives the shocking details.

After Manzanita Spring, the trail gradually climbs to Smith Spring along Smith Canyon, a gorgeous desert riparian zone. On the 0.9-mile trail between the two springs you can observe the aftermath of the 6,012-acre Frijole Fire of 1990, caused by lightning. You can see how some vegetation has made a comeback, but you can also see how slowly nature heals the land in the desert environment.

Smith Spring is a extraordinary oasis in the desert that literally springs out of the permeable limestone of the Guadalupe Mountains. So much water seeps out of the rock that it forms a small waterfall and a live stream.

Smith Spring is shaded by maidenhair fern, bigtooth maple, chinkepin oak and Texas madrone. Imagine a fern in the middle of the Chihuahuan Desert!

The water in Smith Spring certainly looks good enough to drink, but please don't do it. It's against NPS regulations, and the water is unsuitable for human consumption. You get the bonus of leaving Smith Spring by gingerly stepping on well-placed stones to cross the stream with dry feet.

Both Smith and Manzanita springs are very fragile, so please observe at a distance, especially at Smith Spring. Stay in the fenced viewing area.

On the way back to the Frijole Ranch, you get a great view of Manzanita Spring with a distinct, cone-shaped landmark called Nipple Hill as a backdrop.

After 0.9 mile of easy downhill walking, the Frijole Trail heads off to the west. Shortly thereafter, you'll see another junction that heads south to the Foothills Trail. Take a left at both junctions, and after another 0.3 mile you're back in the Frijole Ranch parking lot.

9 FOOTHILLS

Type of trail:	Loop, but could be a short shuttle.
Type of trip:	Day hike.
Total distance:	4.5 miles.
Difficulty:	Moderate.
Elevation change:	640 feet.
Time required:	3-5 hours.
Maps:	Trails Illustrated Guadalupe Mountains Map and USGS Guadalupe Peak and park brochure.
Starting point:	Frijole Ranch or Pine Springs Trailhead.

See Map on Page 77

Key points:
- 0.05 Junction with Foothills Trail.
- 1.9 Junction with Frijole Trail.
- 3.0 Junction with Bear Canyon Trail.
- 4.2 Junction with Smith Spring Trail.
- 4.5 Frijole Ranch.

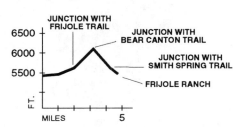

Finding the trailhead: Drive north from the main entrance to Guadalupe Mountains National Park on U.S. Highway 62/180 for 1 mile and turn (left) north. The turn-off is well-signed as "Frijole Ranch." Head up the well-maintained gravel road for about 0.5 mile until it deadends at the historic ranch and museum. You can also start this hike at the Pine Springs Trailhead.

The trail: You can take this loop from either the Frijole Ranch or the Pine Springs Trailhead. However, starting at Pine Springs means 1 mile of additional hiking to get to and from the foothills trail. This trail description follows the clockwise route starting from the Frijole Ranch.

From the Frijole Ranch parking lot, take the main trail heading north from the parking lot and turn left after about 50 feet on to the Foothills Trail as it turns south.

The first 0.6 mile of the trail follows the gravel road heading from U.S Highway 62/180 to the Frijole Ranch. Then, it turns right (west) and parallels the highway, but at a tolerable distance. The roads and the power lines along the first 1.9 miles of this trail may seem like unwelcome distractions, but you can probably forget the intrusions by watching deer, which seem to be everywhere along this trail.

After 1.3 miles of paralleling the highway, you reach the junction with the Frijole Trail. Take a right (north) and start a gradual climb toward the mouth of Bear Canyon. After 1.1 miles, the Bear Canyon Trail climbs northward to the Guadalupe high country. You turn right (east) and stay on the Frijole Trail, which levels out and goes 1.2 miles in the shadow of the escarpment. This is probably the nicest part of the loop. You get good views of the Frijole Ranch and the Pine Springs vicinity. Then, you juncture with the Smith Spring Trail about 0.3 mile from the Frijole Ranch. Turn left, and it's only 0.3 mile to the parking lot.

10 BUSH MOUNTAIN

Type of trail: Loop (actually a "figure eight").
Type of trip: Overnighter, suited for one, two, or three nights out.

See Map on Page 108

Total distance: 17.8 miles.
Difficulty: Difficult.
Elevation change: 2,809 feet.
Time required: At least two full days.
Maps: Trails Illustrated Guadalupe Mountains Map and USGS Guadalupe Peak and PX Flat.
Starting point: Pine Springs Campground.

Key points:

0.05 El Capitan/Guadalupe Peak Trail Junction.
0.1 Frijole Trail Junction.
3.7 Bush Mountain Trail Junction.
3.9 Pine Top Camp.
6.2 Bush Mountain Camp.
6.5 Bush Mountain.
8.4 Blue Ridge Trail Junction.
8.9 Blue Ridge Camp.
10.1 Marcus Trail Junction.
10.4 Tejas Trail Junction.
11.2 Tejas Camp.
11.5 Juniper Trail Junction.
13.0 Bush Mountain Trail Junction.
13.5 The Bowl Trail Junction.
13.9 Spur trail to summit of Hunter Peak.
14.4 Bear Canyon Trail Junction.
16.2 Frijole Trail Junction.
17.3 Foothills Trail Junction.
17.7 Tejas Trail Junction.
17.8 Pine Springs Trailhead.

The salt flats viewed from the Bush Mountain Trail.

The trail: This loop trail offers an ideal multi-day adventure in the remote regions of the Guadalupe Mountains—and also the opportunity to see the most famous features of the park, such as Guadalupe Peak and the "best view in Texas" from the summit of Hunter Peak. This trip has an advantage over other multi-day backpacks in the Guadalupe Mountains. It's a loop and doesn't require shuttling a vehicle to the other trailhead or arranging a ride. Be sure to get your backcountry camping permit before hitting the trail.

Three days and two nights (at Bush Mountain and Tejas camps) is just right for this loop. This splits up nicely into a 6-mile segment for each day.

Well-conditioned hikers on a tight schedule can reduce the trip to two days, staying overnight at the Blue Ridge Camp at approximately the halfway point, but this means two strenuous 9-mile days—especially the first day which is mostly uphill. You can also take four days, staying three nights (probably at Pine Top, Blue Ridge and again at Pine Top), and enjoy a relaxed pace that will give you ample time for side trips and to fully enjoy the Guadalupe high country. In any case, be sure to take plenty of water.

The lower loop of this figure-eight hike is described in detail under the trail description for hike number 6, the Hunter Peak Loop. As with that hike, you could take this hike counterclockwise instead of clockwise, but it would mean a very steep climb up Bear Canyon with a big pack, which is only recommended for hikers who want as much exercise as possible.

The upper loop of the figure eight, however, can be done in either direction. The clockwise route seems only slightly easier because of the gradual climbs as opposed to the shorter, steeper climbs found on the counterclockwise route, especially the climb (about 800 feet in a mile of trail) just east of the Blue Ridge Camp. The clockwise route was used for this trail description.

From the Pine Springs Trailhead, it's a steady uphill grind to the top of the escarpment, accounting for most of the elevation gain on this multi-day trip (almost 2,000 feet in 3.7 miles). From this point on, you can expect only minor elevation gain and short hills. At this point, you're entering the "high country," and you remain there the rest of the trip until you plunge down Bear Canyon.

If you started late in the day and plan at least a two-night trip, you can stay at Pine Top Camp, 0.2 mile to your left on the Bush Mountain Trail just beyond the junction you'll find immediately after cresting the rim of the escarpment. Pine Top Camp has six tent sites and a great view.

If you started early in the day and plan two nights out, you might want to push on to the Bush Mountain Camp, which has five tent sites and is nestled under a grove of huge Douglas-fir and ponderosa pine, but lacks the scenic vista found at Pine Top.

From the top of the escarpment, the Bush Mountain Trail climbs steadily for the first mile, gaining about 500 feet. It closely follows the steep edge of Pine Springs Canyon, offering incredible views of the expansive canyon and Guadalupe, Shumard, and Bartlett peaks.

The trail continues to climb, gradually, past Bush Mountain Camp, to the top of 8,631-foot Bush Mountain, the second highest peak in the park and all of Texas. The high-country forest stays with you all the way, even as you crest the summit of Bush Mountain, making the climb seem gentle. The serenity of the wilderness is broken briefly by a misplaced radio repeater station on top of Bush Mountain. However, you can quickly forget that minor intrusion by soaking in the extraordinary view of the salt flats, nearly 4,000 feet below, from an overlook near the top of Bush Mountain.

About 1.9 miles past the summit of Bush Mountain, you hit the Blue Ridge Trail Junction. Turn right (east) here and go another 0.5 mile to the Blue Ridge Camp on your left. If you're out for only one night, this is your best campsite. Like Bush Mountain camp, Blue Ridge Camp is shaded by stately Douglas-fir and ponderosa pine, plus a few large oak trees. It has only two tent sites, but this camp gets little use, so you probably won't have trouble getting a permit to stay here.

From Bush Mountain Camp, all along the Blue Ridge Trail, and on to the Tejas Camp, you hike through the diversity of the relict forest of the Guadalupe Mountains. Watch for deer, elk, turkey, and other wildlife along the way—or take an early morning or late evening stroll from camp when the local residents are more active.

After a mile or so of fairly level—and very enjoyable—hiking on the Blue Ridge, you drop down a steep, rocky section to the Marcus Trail Junction where you go straight (east) and continue on another 0.3 mile to the Tejas Trail. Here, turn right (south) on the Tejas Trail and go another 0.8 mile to the Tejas Camp, following a beautiful (and usually dry) streambed much of the way.

If you're out for two nights, the Tejas Camp is probably your best choice for a second campsite. The Tejas Camp has four tent sites, with number 1 offering the best view.

After leaving the Tejas Camp, you quickly reach the junction with the Juniper Trail. You can take this alternative route back to Bear Canyon, but you'll miss Hunter Peak. So, turn right at this junction and drop into the streambed for about a half mile before climbing out into the high-country forest all the way back to the center of your figure-eight route, the junction with the Bush Mountain and Bowl trails. At this junction, you can bail out early and head back down the Tejas Trail to Pine Springs, but this only cuts a mile off your trip, and you'll miss some of the best scenery. So, instead, turn left (east) and follow the Bowl Trail along the rim of the escarpment past Hunter Peak for 1.4 miles to the Bear Canyon Junction.

After 0.5 mile on the Bowl Trail, it splits. You continue going east along the edge of the cliff. Be sure to make a lengthy stop at Hunter Peak. Watch for the spur trail heading off to the right 0.4 mile after Bowl Trail splits and then another 0.5 mile to the Bear Canyon Junction. From here, it's all downhill back to the Pine Springs Trailhead. Refer to the Hunter Peak Loop trail description for more details.

11 PINE SPRINGS TO MCKITTRICK CANYON

Type of trail:	Shuttle.
Type of trip:	Overnighter.
Total distance:	18.9 miles.
Difficulty:	Moderate, but long.
Elevation change:	1,978 feet.
Time required:	Best suited for a three-day trip, but could be done in two.
Maps:	Trails Illustrated Guadalupe Mountains Map and USGS Guadalupe Peak.
Starting point:	Pine Springs Campground.

Key points:
0.05 Junction with Guadalupe Peak and El Capitan Trails.
0.1 Junction with Tejas Trail.
3.7 Junction with Bush Mountain and Bowl Trails.
5.2 Junction with Juniper Trail.
5.5 Tejas Camp.
6.3 Junction with Blue Ridge Trail.
7.0 Mescalero Camp.
7.8 Junction with McKittrick Canyon Trail.
11.3 McKittrick Ridge Camp.
14.0 The Notch.
15.4 Spur Trail to The Grotto and Hunter Line Cabin.
16.5 Pratt Lodge.
18.9 McKittrick Canyon Trailhead and Visitor Center.

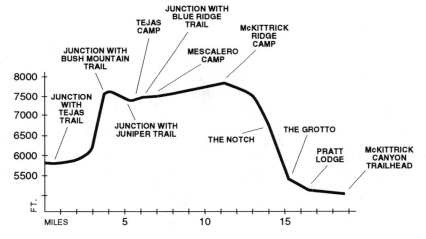

Stepping stones in McKittrick Canyon Creek help preserve water quality.

The trail: This trail slices through the heart of the Guadalupe Mountains and exposes many of its famous jewels to hikers lucky enough to take the trip. It includes views of Guadalupe Peak, a great walk in the woods through the relict high-altitude forest, vistas from the summit of Hunter Peak and McKittrick Canyon's famed viewpoint called "The Notch," and the historic lodges and the natural wonders of McKittrick Canyon. If you have three days to see the Guadalupe Mountains, you couldn't spend the time much better.

You could do this trip in two days, but they would be two long days. This trail description covers the three-day, two-night option.

The first step is arranging transportation. The best option is leaving a vehicle at McKittrick Canyon Visitor Center. Because of the arduous climb to the top of McKittrick Ridge coming from the other direction, you won't want to do this trip in reverse. The big climb also makes it marginal for the "trading keys" option because a fight would likely break out over who has to start at the McKittrick Canyon Trailhead.

When transportation has been arranged and you've obtained your backcountry camping permit, start your adventure at the Pine Springs Trailhead. Immediately beyond Pine Springs Campground, turn right on the Frijole Trail at the major junction with trails going off to the left to Guadalupe Peak and El Capitan and straight to Devil's Hall. Then, in another 0.25 mile, after crossing the large dry wash of Pine Springs Canyon, you hit another junction with the Tejas Trail. Turn left and head north up the hill on the Tejas Trail.

The next mile is nearly flat with an almost indiscernible increase in elevation. Then, you start a moderate climb to Pine Top, gaining almost 2,000 feet over 3 miles of well-designed trail that minimizes the impact of the climb. This trail is as good as a trail can be, but it still doesn't make this an easy hike, especially on a hot day with your big pack heavy with a three-day water supply.

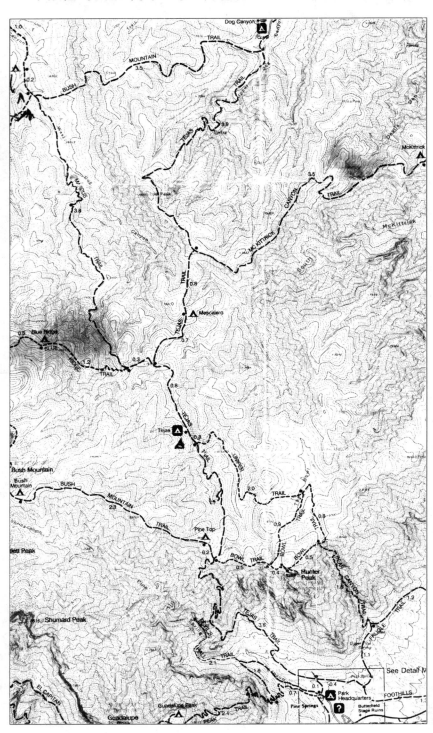

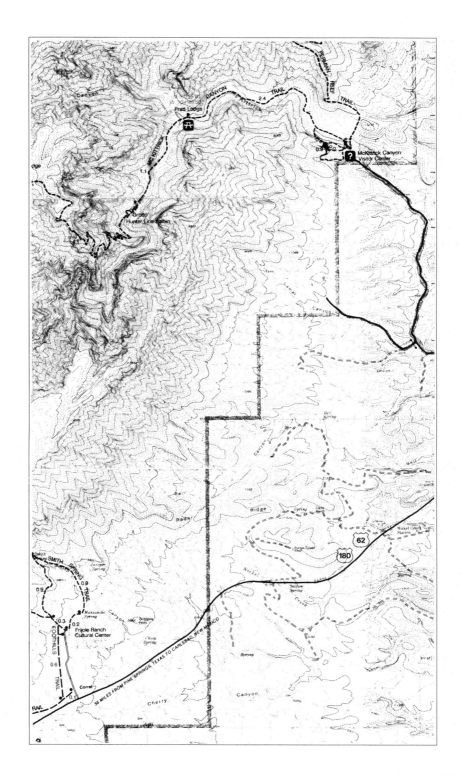

Depending on how late in the day you hit the trail and the availability of backcountry permits, you have the choice of spending the first night at Pine Top or Tejas camps. Tejas Camp is better situated at 5.5 miles into your hike, leaving 5.8 miles and 7.6 miles respectively for the second and third day of the trip. If you stay at Pine Top, you leave 7.6 miles for each of the last two days of the trip.

Pine Top Camp has six tent sites and a great view. Tejas Camp has four tent sites, and the view doesn't match that of Pine Top. To reach Pine Top Camp, you climb 0.2 mile to the left on the Bush Mountain Trail when you reach the junction at the rim of the escarpment—and then retrace your steps to the junction the next morning, lengthening your trip by about a half mile.

The trail between the two camps passes through the deep forest of the Guadalupe Mountains as it gradually descends to Tejas Camp. Just before Tejas camp, you'll see the Juniper Trail veering off to the right. You go straight (north), staying on the Tejas Trail.

About 0.8 mile beyond Tejas Camp, the Blue Ridge Trail branches off to the left. Stay on the Tejas Trail. In another 0.7 mile you'll see the Mescalero Camp on your right. This is a great campsite with eight tent sites, but it's poorly located for a three-day trip. For a two-day trip, the Mescalero Camp would be your best choice for your overnight stay.

In 0.8 mile, you reach the junction with the McKittrick Canyon Trail. Here, you leave the Tejas Trail and turn right (east) on the McKittrick Canyon Trail. From Pine Top to the McKittrick Trail Junction, the trail has stayed in the forest, but on McKittrick Ridge the forest opens up and treats you to magnificent vistas in all directions for the next 5 miles. On your right, you have the complete wildness of South McKittrick Canyon, which has been totally preserved by the NPS with no entry allowed.

Along the way, about 3.5 miles after the junction, you'll see the McKittrick Ridge Camp on your left, your campsite for the second night out. McKittrick Ridge Camp has eight tent sites. Numbers 1 and 8 offer the most privacy. About the only place on McKittrick Ridge where you can't get a great view is from the camp that is off the trail in a fairly dense stand of junipers, Douglas-fir and ponderosa pine.

After you leave McKittrick Ridge Camp the next morning, it's all downhill. You stay on the ridge for about 1.5 miles and then, start down the big drop into the colorful bottomlands of McKittrick Canyon. Here is where you're glad you took the author's advice and didn't do the trip in reverse.

While hiking through McKittrick Canyon, be sure to stop at The Grotto and Hunter Line Cabin about 4 miles from the camp and Pratt Lodge another mile down the trail. Just before Pratt Lodge, you're suddenly exposed to a very rare sight in the Guadalupe Mountains—a free-flowing stream that surfaces here and there along the last 3 miles of the trail. This stream is an extremely precious resource, and park regulations prohibit entering the stream or using the water for any reason. You can usually get drinking water at Pratt Lodge.

The entire trip through McKittrick Canyon passes through a lush and diverse forest quite unlike the high-altitude forest of the Bowl. You'll definitely feel nature saved the best part for last, especially if you do this trip in the fall with McKittrick Canyon awash with the colors of autumn. Be sure to stay on the trail. Park regulations prohibit off-trail travel in McKittrick Canyon.

The McKittrick Canyon road closes at 6 p.m. while daylight savings time is in effect and 4:30 p.m. during standard time., so you must be out of the woods and on the road in time to reach U.S. Highway 62/180 before the NPS locks the gate.

MCKITTRICK CANYON TRAILHEAD

McKittrick Canyon shows up on lots of postcards and photo essays. It's a truly exquisite place and has even been called "the most beautiful spot in Texas."

As you drive by on U.S. Highway 62/180, you probably won't notice the mouth of the canyon. In fact, the hidden beauty of the canyon doesn't reveal itself until you're almost in it. A heavily used trail follows the streambed and then climbs out of the canyon and into the heart of the Guadalupe Mountains.

Named after Felix McKittrick who ran cattle in the canyon around 1870, the canyon now endures as a tiny island of untamed nature. You can buy a brochure at the visitor center that fully explains the history of McKittrick Canyon.

The canyon is revered by photographers who flock there in the fall when the maple, oak, and ash trees are ablaze with color. But the most unusual natural phenomenon of all is the permanent, spring-fed stream flowing out of the canyon—very rare in this arid corner of the world. Rainbow trout were introduced into the stream, and it now supports a viable population.

The canyon is also famous for its diversity of plants and animals. For example, 58 mammals and 260 birds have been seen in McKittrick Canyon, not to mention the unbelievable diversity of vegetation, a unique melding of high-altitude and desert plants. The canyon has gathered plants from all environments. It isn't just one beautiful place; it's part of several beautiful places.

It's also a fragile place. The NPS has imposed many regulations to protect it—no overnight camping, no pets, no wading in the stream, etc. Hikers must stay on the trail, and after the Grotto, no entry at all is allowed in South McKittrick Canyon to completely protect it. McKittrick Canyon is an uncommon and naturally precious place. These regulations will keep it that way.

FINDING THE TRAILHEAD

To find the trailhead, go north from the park headquarters at Pine Springs on U.S. Highway 62/180 for 8 miles until you see the well-signed turn into McKittrick Canyon. Turn west at this turn and follow the paved road 4.5 miles to the McKittrick Canyon Visitor Center parking lot. The trails start behind the visitor center.

Type of trail:	Loop
Type of trip:	Day hike.
Total distance:	0.9 mile.
Difficulty:	Easy.
Elevation change:	Minimal.
Time required:	1 hour.
Maps:	Trails Illustrated Guadalupe Mountains Map and USGS Guadalupe Peak and Independence Spring and the park brochure.
Starting point:	McKittrick Canyon Visitor Center.

The trail: This trail is just right for a short, easy hike. Along the way you get a bonus—a chance to learn about many plants and animals inhabiting the McKittrick Canyon area.

The trail starts right at the visitor center. Take a left at the junction just past the center. In addition to seeing some great scenery at the entrance to the grand McKittrick Canyon, you learn all kinds of things—and enjoy doing it.

You'll learn why you should like rattlesnakes, how the oversized soaptree yucca depends on a tiny moth, that alligator juniper can grow as old as 800 years in this harsh environment, how javelina depend on prickly pear pads for food and water, the favorite food of the local deer population, and the facts about the "century plant."

About twenty more interpretive signs tell you even more. You'll love this classroom.

McKittrick Canyon Nature Trail
McKittrick Canyon • McKittrick Ridge
Permian Reef

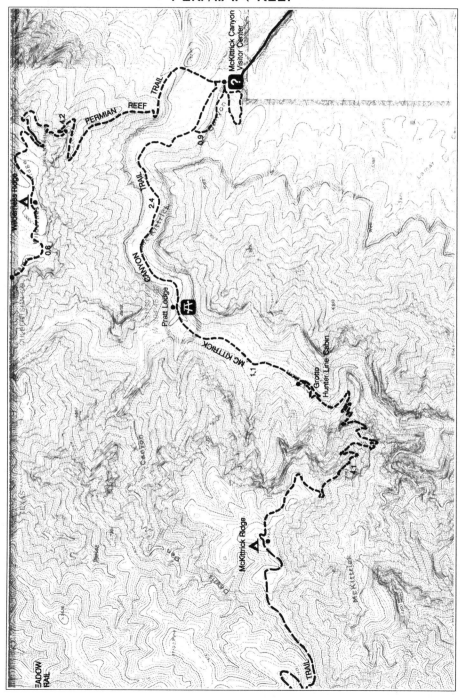

13 MCKITTRICK CANYON

Type of trail: Out and back.

See Map on Page 97

Type of trip: Day hike.

Total distance: 4.6 miles to Pratt Lodge,
7 miles to The Grotto; 10.2 miles to The Notch.

Difficulty: Easy to Pratt Lodge; moderate to The Grotto; and difficult to the Notch.

Elevation change: 200 feet to Pratt Lodge, 340 feet to The Grotto; and about 1,300 feet to The Notch.

Time required: 3-5 hours to Pratt Lodge, 4-6 hours to The Grotto; and 5-8 hours to The Notch.

Maps: Trails Illustrated Guadalupe Mountains Map and USGS Guadalupe Peak and Independence Spring and the park brochure.

Starting point: McKittrick Canyon Visitor Center.

Key points:

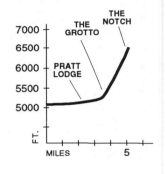

  2.3 Pratt Lodge

  3.4 Junction with spur trail to The Grotto and Hunter Line Cabin.

  3.5 The Grotto and Hunter Line Cabin

  4.0 Start of the big climb.

  5.1 The Notch.

The trail: As you drive up the road toward McKittrick Canyon, you might not believe you're headed for one of most famous and scenic spots in Texas. The topography hides the canyon well.

Rest assured that McKittrick Canyon is a truly wonderful place, but don't plan on having it to yourself. This is probably is the most popular hike in the Guadalupe Mountains—and with good reason.

The trail meanders through a spectacular forest with a wide variety of conifers and deciduous trees. During autumn, the maples, oaks, and other hardwoods burst into a world-famous kaleidoscopic panorama of fall colors. The trees are the same species found in other canyons in the park, but here, they're bigger, and the entire forest seems more lush and majestic in the shadow of the steep cliffs on both sides of the canyon.

Hikers also get the rare opportunity to walk along a permanent desert stream—with a reproducing trout population. The stream appears and disappears several places along the first 3 miles of this hike. Please don't drink or wade in the stream. It's so special and rare and fragile that everybody must take the greatest care not to despoil it even in the slightest way.

About 2.3 miles up the trail, hikers can marvel at the grand old Pratt Lodge, so stately and nicely situated at the confluence of North McKittrick Canyon and South McKittrick Canyon that it inspires dreams of spending a few nights in this paradise,

View of McKittrick Canyon from the Notch.

The first part of the excellent trail up McKittrick Canyon.

but sorry, the lodge is closed to the public. However, NPS volunteers often stay there to take care of the lodge and answer your questions—a "tough job" if you can afford it.

The first part of trail is in embarrassingly good condition, double wide all the way and flat. It "climbs" inch-by-inch for a total of only 200 feet elevation over 2.3 miles. The trail crosses the flowing stream twice on the way to Pratt Lodge.

The lodge is named for Wallace E. Pratt a young geologist for Humble Oil Company (now Exxon) who built the residence at the scenic confluence of North and South McKittrick Canyons in the 1920s and 1930s. He and his family lived there off and on until 1957 when they donated 5,632 acres of their 16,000-acre ranch to the U.S. government for the beginnings of a national park.

Pratt Lodge is a large stone building with several outbuildings. Of special note are the magnificent stone picnic tables and a historic stone fence surrounding the lodge. You can get drinking water at the Lodge (except from mid-November to early March), but be sure to verify this at the visitor center before you hit the trail without water.

Beyond the lodge, the trail gets "normal." The stream surfaces again just down the trail from the lodge. The trail continues through the same forested environs for another 1.1 mile until a spur trail veers off to your left. Take this trail for about 0.1 mile to The Grotto which is akin to a "surface cave" complete with speleoderms that look like they should be subterranean. This is also a good place for a lunch break on one of the stone picnic tables found there.

Just down the spur trail from The Grotto, you see the historic Hunter Line Cabin where the spur trail ends. The cabin served as temporary quarters for ranch hands working the large Guadalupe Mountains Ranch owned by Judge J. C. Hunter and his son J.C. Hunter, Jr. After the Hunter family sold to the NPS, it became a major portion of the park.

South McKittrick Canyon beyond the Hunter Line Cabin has been preserved by the NPS as a Research Natural Area with no entry allowed. If you're heading to The Notch, retrace your steps to the main trail and head up the canyon.

In a half mile or so, you reach the bottom of the toughest climb in Guadalupe Mountains National Park. The 2,600-foot ascent rivals any hill in the park, even the trip up to the summit of Guadalupe Peak. On a hot day, you'll be glad you aren't carrying a big pack.

The trail switchbacks up the side of South McKittrick Canyon for about 1.5 miles, until it slips through a distinctive narrow spot in the cliff called The Notch. This is a perfect place to take a long break and absorb the extraordinary scenery you probably didn't notice as you climbed up here. Now, you can sit down and look back down the canyon and see the Hunter Line Cabin, Pratt Lodge, and the multi-splendored forest surrounding them. The view is just as staggering as the trip up was. When you think about how hard it was to get to the Notch, you realize that you've only covered about half of the climb to the top of McKittrick Ridge.

After relaxing for awhile, retrace your steps back to the visitor center. Be sure to leave enough time to get out to U.S. Hwy. 62/180, as the NPS closes the gate at 6 p.m. MDT and 4:30 p.m. MST.

14 MCKITTRICK RIDGE

Type of trail: Out and back.
Type of trip: Overnighter.
Total distance: 15.2 miles.
Difficulty: Easy to Pratt Lodge; moderate to The Grotto; and difficult the rest of the way.
Elevation change: 2,736 feet.
Time required: 5-8 hours going in, 3-5 hours coming out.
Maps: Trails Illustrated Guadalupe Mountains Map and USGS Guadalupe Peak and Independence Spring.
Starting point: McKittrick Canyon Visitor Center.

See Map on Page 97

Key points:
2.3 Pratt Lodge
3.4 Junction with spur trail to The Grotto and Hunter Line Cabin.
3.5 The Grotto and Hunter Line Cabin.
4.0 Start of the big climb.
5.1 The Notch.
7.6 McKittrick Ridge Camp.

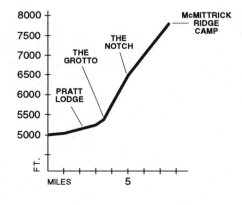

The trail: For a more detailed description of the first part of this hike, refer to the McKittrick Canyon trail description. The first part of this trip follows the same trail up to The Grotto. Be sure to get a backcountry camping permit at the visitor center before you hit the trail.

Shortly after The Grotto, the trail changes dramatically. It's no longer the serene walk in the woods of the McKittrick Canyon bottomlands. It's quite the other extreme.

After about 3.6 miles of easy walking, the trail starts climbing up what could be called "The Big Sweat." It's as steep of a climb as you'll find on any established trail. You gain about 2,300 feet in elevation in about 4 miles. Most of this elevation gain (about 1,600 feet) occurs in the first 1.5 miles. The grade eases slightly after you go through The Notch, where the trail passes through a distinctive narrowing of the canyon walls.

Steps carved out of solid rock help hikers get up the big hill to McKittrick Ridge.

The Hunter Line Cabin.

Since the climb starts 3.6 miles from the trailhead, it's difficult to do early in the morning to take advantage of cooler temperatures. Therefore, unfortunately, it's usually hot and always steep. This means you need to carry lots of water.

It's a vicious circle. You need to carry lots of water, which makes your pack heavier, which means you go slower and work harder, which means you dip into the hottest part of the day, which means you sweat more, which means you need to carry lots of water.

It's best to plan for a whole day on the trail. Go slowly and take lots of rest stops to take in the scenery, which is fantastic. From several points on the trail, you can marvel at the size and beauty of McKittrick Canyon.

After about 2.5 miles you lose some of your view into McKittrick Canyon, as the trail slips into a forested environment. You're still climbing, though, but not as steeply, for another 1.5 miles or so until you see the McKittrick Ridge Camp on your right.

The McKittrick Ridge Camp has eight tent sites with number 1 and 8 offering the most privacy. You don't get the same panoramic view from the camp as you had the last half of your hike up to the camp, but you can satisfy that need by hiking down the trail to the west for another 100 yards or so. The camp itself is nestled in a beautiful grove of ponderosa pine, Douglas-fir and junipers.

If you have any energy left after supper, take a short hike on the trail west from the camp along the ridgeline. The scenery is sensational, and you'll probably see deer and elk enjoying the last hours of sunlight.

After a relaxing evening and a good night's sleep at the McKittrick Ridge Camp, retrace your steps back to the visitor center the next morning. Be sure to leave camp early enough to get out to U.S. Highway 62\180, as the NPS closes the gate at 6 p.m. MDT or 4:30 p.m. MST.

15 PERMIAN REEF

Type of trail:	Out and back.
Type of trip:	Day hike or overnighter.
Total distance:	8.4 miles.
Difficulty:	Difficult.
Elevation change:	2,202 feet.
Time required:	5-8 hours.
Maps:	Trails Illustrated Guadalupe Mountains Map and USGS Guadalupe Peak and Independence Spring and park brochure.
Starting point:	McKittrick Canyon Visitor Center.

See Map on Page 97

Key points:

0.1 Trail leaves dry wash.
3.5 Wilderness Ridge.
4.2 Wilderness Ridge Camp.
4.8 Park boundary.

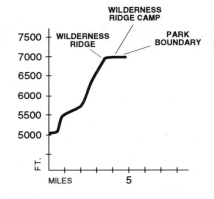

The trail: Permian Reef is one of the most spectacular trails in the park. Yet, it doesn't receive much use. Most people going to McKittrick Canyon to hike choose the flat route up the beautiful, forested canyon, and who can blame them when the alternative is a 2,000-foot climb to Wilderness Ridge? For somebody who wants more exercise, though, this trail may be just as rewarding—and definitely less crowded. It can be a wonderful day-long hike or a great overnighter. If you're spending the night at the Wilderness Ridge Camp, be sure to get a permit at the visitor center before leaving.

The trail does get heavy use from geology fans. In fact, the University of Texas-El Paso has a cooperative arrangement with the NPS to use the trail as an outdoor classroom. Key geological points are marked on the trail with 28 metal signs. You can learn more about the geological story of the area by purchasing a book on the area at one of the park's visitor centers.

The trail starts out just past the visitor center. Take a right at the trail register and follow an old road for about a 100 yards through and along the dry wash of McKittrick Canyon Creek, until you see the sign where the Permian Reef Trail starts switchbacking up the canyon wall. The trail is very well-constructed to minimize the impact of the climb, so if you're in good shape, you'll barely notice the elevation gain. There is one section about two-thirds of the way up where the trail is etched out of the steep canyon wall. This section might be nerve-wracking for parents with young children.

After you've climbed for awhile, you can look down into McKittrick Canyon and clearly see where the stream suddenly disappears into the streambed, appears again momentarily, and then disappears again.

After a mile or so, on a little plateau, you'll see a Geology Loop Trail veering off to the right. This is a special trail used for geology classes, so take a left, staying on the main route. The loop re-joins the main route a short way up the trail.

Between markers 4 and 5, the trail goes through a narrow slot. And at about the 2.5-mile point just past marker 15, it looks like you've reached the top of the ridge, but, sorry, it's a false summit. You're only slightly more than halfway to the ridgeline.

At about the 3.5-mile mark, you break out onto Wilderness Ridge, and the trail is flat the rest of the way. The vistas up here will stop you in your tracks.

Wilderness Ridge Camp is on your right amid a few scattered ponderosa pines and junipers. It has five tent sites, and the scenery rivals any camp in the park. Beauty is always in the eye of the beholder, but this camp along with Guadalupe Peak Camp, would probably be voted most scenic in the park by anybody who has seen all of them.

If you're staying overnight, take a hike that evening or the next morning for another 0.6 mile along Wilderness Ridge to the park boundary. The trail worsens slightly because of lack of use, but it's a beautiful walk. If you want more hiking, you can continue on outside of the park into the Lincoln National Forest.

Be sure you leave enough time to get down to the visitor center and then out to U.S. Highway 62/180 before 6 p.m. MDT or 4:30 p.m. MST when the NPS locks the gate.

DOG CANYON TRAILHEAD

Located just south of the New Mexico/Texas line, the Dog Canyon Campground and Trailhead is a remote jewel on the north edge of Guadalupe Mountains National Park. The other two trailheads (Pine Springs and McKittrick Canyon) receive heavy use, mainly because they are right along U.S. Highway 62/180. On the other hand, you have to put in some extra miles and effort to get to Dog Canyon. If you have an extra day, however, it's worth the trip.

The campground itself is a delightful combination of modern convenience and primitive beauty. You'll find a water fountain and toilet facilities, but there is also a nice array of native vegetation around the 15 tent sites and more privacy than you might normally find in a developed campground. The campground has parking spots for recreational vehicles (no hook-ups) and is used by both backpackers for overnight stays and tent campers who drive the 70 miles from Carlsbad, New Mexico. The trailhead is about 100 yards south of the campground.

You can usually see deer right from the tent sites, and if you get up early, you'll see the grand exodus of the local turkey vulture population, which roosts overnight on big snags just east of the campground.

Early settlers named this place Dog Canyon for the high population of black-tailed prairie dogs in the area. However, the unpopular rodents were exterminated long ago.

In 1994, a lightning-caused fire burnt much of the area west of the campground. However, nature is rapidly reclaiming the area.

FINDING THE TRAILHEAD

From Carlsbad, New Mexico, go north on U.S. Highway 285 for about 12 miles and turn left (west) on New Mexico Highway 137. Stay on NM 137 for about 58 miles until in ends at the Dog Canyon Campground.

Type of trail:	Loop.
Type of trip:	Short day hike.
Total distance:	0.6 mile.
Difficulty:	Easy.
Elevation change:	Minimal.
Time required:	30-45 minutes.
Maps:	No map needed; use brochure available at trailhead.
Starting point:	Dog Canyon Campground.

See Map on Page 108

The trail: The Indian Meadow Nature Trail can be found by following a groomed trail (a 5 -minute walk) south from the water fountain in Dog Canyon Campground.

Early settlers in the area saw tepees set up in this meadow and named it Indian Meadow. Today, it's certainly easy to see why Native Americans used the meadow as a campsite. It's level, protected, and near water sources.

This isn't really a hike. It's an evening or early morning stroll that offers an educational bonus—a series of 25 designated stops keyed to a free interpretive brochure available at the trailhead. The brochure describes the remarkable natural diversity of the area as well as its cultural history. It's certainly rare to be able to study so many aspects of natural and cultural history in one small spot—and in such a convenient location. This is a dirt trail with no hills, perfect for hikers interested in a short, easy stroll or for people unable to walk long distances.

You learn about native vegetation such as red berberis, alligator juniper, ponderosa pine, cane cholla, prickly pear, and desert rose; how the plants provide vital food and habitat for birds and mammals; how to watch for fascinating micro-habitats; how water (or lack thereof) affects local plants and animals; how the area formed geologically; and how early residents and settlers adapted to the area.

As in all parts of the park, don't damage or collect any natural features. This is particularly important here, as so many people use this trail. If each person took one rock or flower, it would rapidly deface the gorgeous meadow.

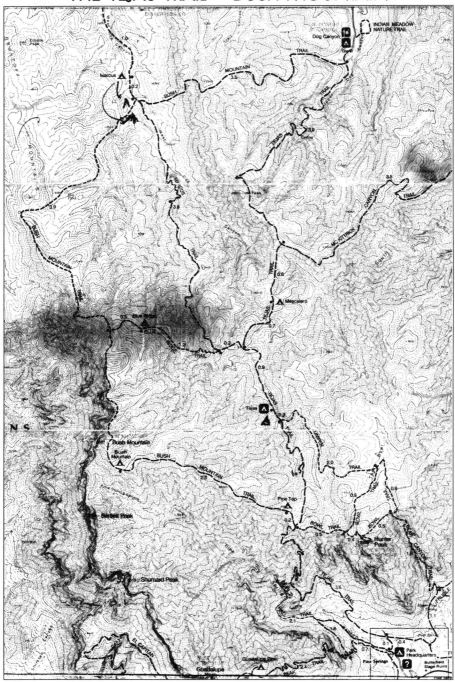

17 LOST PEAK

Type of trail:	Out and back.
Type of trip:	Day hike.
Total distance:	6 miles.
Difficulty:	Moderate.
Elevation change:	1,420 feet.
Time required:	3-5 hours.
Maps:	Trails Illustrated Guadalupe Mountains Map and USGS Guadalupe Peak and the park brochure.
Starting point:	Dog Canyon Trailhead.

The trail: For people staying at Dog Canyon Campground, the Indian Meadow Interpretive Trail may not be enough exercise and excitement. If so, the Lost Peak trail is a great choice for a half-day hike. It's a convenient distance (6 miles), and with a 1,400-foot elevation gain in 3 miles, you'll get enough exercise.

In 1994, a lightning-caused fire scorched much of the area right around the campground. You can see that nature has quickly reclaimed the surface, but it will take many years to replace some of the majestic trees killed in the fire.

The junction with the Marcus Trail veers off to the right just after you leave the Dog Canyon Trailhead. You go left and follow the Tejas Trail. Even though some sections of this trail were burned, it's still a pleasant hike, especially at dawn and dusk when the local residents (wild turkey, deer, and other wild animals) are out in force.

The trail gradually climbs for the first 1.5 miles, following Dog Canyon. Just before you get to Dog Canyon Springs, the trail takes a sharp right and starts a steep climb up to Lost Peak. Then, you switchback up the west side of Dog Canyon and to a ridgeline where you get great views back into the campground area you just left. You gain most elevation in the next 1.5 miles, about 1,100 feet if you go all the way to the top of Lost Peak.

Watch your topo map, so you don't hike right by Lost Peak. There's no sign. You'll notice it off to your right a short distance off the trail. You can scramble up to the top for the big view and then retrace your steps back to Dog Canyon Trailhead.

18 BLUE RIDGE

Type of trail: Loop.
Type of trip: Overnighter.
Total distance: 14.8 miles.
Difficulty: Difficult.
Elevation change: 1,960 feet.
Time required: Two full days.
Maps: Trails Illustrated Guadalupe Mountains Map and USGS Guadalupe Peak and PX Flat.
Starting point: Dog Canyon Trailhead.

See Map on Page 108

Key points:
- 0.1 Junction with Bush Mountain Trail.
- 1.5 Dog Canyon Spring.
- 3.0 Lost Peak.
- 3.9 Junction with McKittrick Ridge Trail.
- 4.7 Mescalero Camp.
- 5.4 Junction with Blue Ridge Trail.
- 5.7 Junction with Marcus Trail.
- 6.9 Blue Ridge Camp.
- 7.4 Junction with Bush Mountain Trail.
- 11.1 Marcus Camp.
- 11.3 Junction with Marcus Trail.
- 12.8 Divide between West Dog Canyon and Dog Canyon.
- 14.8 Dog Canyon Trailhead.

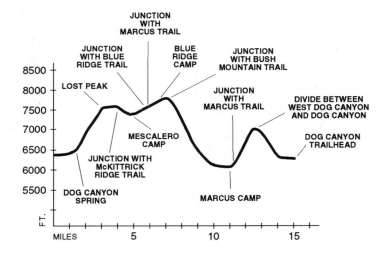

The trail: This trail is for the adventurous hiker only. It goes through the most remote and rugged part of Guadalupe Mountains National Park. You can get your backcountry camping permit at the Dog Canyon Ranger Station just north of the trailhead.

This trip could be done in one very long day of strenuous walking, but this would be too much for most hikers. Instead, take it more slowly and enjoy it by making this an overnighter. For an even more relaxed pace, spend three nights out, each at a different backcountry campsite. To save the steepest and most rugged parts of the loop to the end of the trip, take the clockwise route as described here.

Shortly after leaving Dog Canyon Trailhead, you'll see the Bush Mountain Trail coming in from the right (west). You'll be dragging down this trail on your way out.

Turn left (south) on the Tejas Trail, which follows a burnt, but still beautiful, riparian zone along Dog Canyon for about 1.5 miles to Dog Canyon Springs. Here, the trail takes a sharp right and starts to switchback up toward Lost Peak. After another 1.5 miles you go by Lost Peak on your right. This is a good spot to drop your pack and scramble up to the top for a great view and a needed rest.

In another mile or so, you hit the junction with the McKittrick Canyon Trail coming in from the left (east). Take a right, staying on the Tejas Trail.

If staying out three nights, you'll want to stop at the Mescalero Camp, another 0.8 mile down the trail on your left. Mescalero Camp has eight tent sites, with number 1 the best room in the inn.

If you're staying only one night, however, you'll want to blow by Mescalero Camp and head for Blue Ridge Camp. You'll see the junction with the Blue Ridge Trail about

Looking south toward Bush Mountain, the wildest and roughest part of Guadalupe Mountains National Park.

The Blue Ridge Trail.

0.7 mile past Mescalero Camp. Turn right (west) and start climbing up to Blue Ridge. In 0.5 mile you see the Marcus Trail heading off to the right (north). Keep going west (and climbing) to the Blue Ridge Trail for another 1.2 mile, until you see the Blue Ridge Camp on your right. The first 0.5 mile past the junction with the Marcus Trail is a serious climb—short but steep on a rocky trail with a series of tight switchbacks.

If you're out for only one night, this is your best campsite. The Blue Ridge Camp is shaded by stately Douglas-fir and ponderosa pine, plus a few large oak trees. It has only two tent sites, but this camp gets little use, so you probably won't have trouble getting a permit to stay here.

After a pleasant night on the Blue Ridge, the tough hiking begins. For another scenic 0.5 mile, you continue to straddle the Blue Ridge. Then, take a right at the junction with the Bush Mountain Trail.

Shortly after this junction, you enter the burn of the 1994 Marcus Fire, and the trail gets rough and rocky and, at times, hard to find. For a long stretch of this trail, only cairns and a few NPS brown trail markers mark the way. This trail traditionally received minimal use, so it was not as well-defined as most other trails in the park. Then, the fire made it even more difficult to find.

Try to look at the fire as a natural phenomenon instead of a destructive force. Also, look at it as a short-term distraction. Fire is an essential part of nature, and in many cases, it's essential to the long-term health of the area's fauna and flora.

As you head down toward West Dog Canyon, you'll be happy with your decision to take the clockwise route. The trail drops steeply after leaving the Blue Ridge, and you wouldn't want to climb this hill with a big pack.

If you want to be alone, this is the place. Very few hikers use this trail compared to others in the park.

After about 1.5 miles, the trail levels off and goes through open, gently rolling country all the way to West Dog Canyon. Before this area became a national park it was ranchland, and even today, you can see signs of the past—old fences, tanks, and the remains of ranch buildings.

Just before you reach the Marcus Trail coming down West Dog Canyon, watch for the Marcus Camp off to your right. If you're out for three nights, this is your third campsite.

You'll find the junction with the Marcus Trail right in the bottom of West Dog Canyon. Take a good break here, because the next 1.5 miles up to the divide between West Dog Canyon and Dog Canyon will be the toughest climb of the entire trip. Besides being steep, this section of trail is rough and rocky. On top, finally, you'll find a hitching rail for horses and a great view. Even better is the news that it's a gradual downhill the last 2 miles back to the Dog Canyon Trailhead.

19 THE MARCUS TRAIL

Type of trail: Loop.
Type of trip: Long day hike or overnighter.
Total distance: 13.1 miles.
Difficulty: Difficult.
Elevation change: 1,530 feet.
Time required: 8-10 hours.
Maps: Trails Illustrated Guadalupe Mountains Map and USGS Guadalupe Peak and the park brochure.
Starting point: Dog Canyon Trailhead.

See Map on Page 108

Key points:

0.1 Junction with Bush Mountain Trail.
2.5 Divide between Dog Canyon and West Dog Canyon.
3.5 West Dog Canyon and junction with Marcus Trail.
7.4 Junction with Blue Ridge Trail.
7.7 Junction with the Tejas Trail.
8.4 Mescalero Camp.
9.2 Junction with McKittrick Ridge Trail.
10.0 Lost Peak.
13.1 Dog Canyon Trailhead.

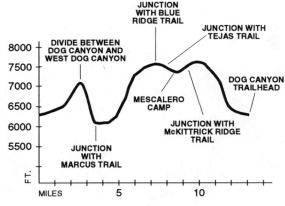

The trail: If you hike this loop counterclockwise (as described here), you can avoid the precipitous 1.5-mile climb up from West Dog Canyon to the divide between West Dog Canyon and Dog Canyon. If you stay overnight at Mescalero Camp, this makes the first day a rough 8.4-mile hike, but it saves you the pain of climbing this steep pitch with an overnight pack.

Whichever way you hike it, however, it's still a long 13.1 miles with a 1,500-foot elevation gain. You can make it a long day hike or take your time and stay overnight at Mescalero Camp. You can get your backcountry permit at the Dog Canyon Ranger Station just north of the trailhead.

Shortly after you leave the Dog Canyon Trailhead on the Tejas Trail, you reach the junction with the Bush Mountain Trail. Turn right (west) on the Bush Mountain Trail. You'll be coming down the Tejas Trail at the end of your hike.

In about 2 miles, a moderately steep climb through the 1994 burn, you top out on the divide between Dog Canyon and West Dog Canyon. Up to this point, the trail is in great shape, but it turns steep and rocky as you crest the divide and head down to West Dog Canyon. This can be difficult footing with a big pack, but you'll be overjoyed you aren't climbing up this hill.

At the bottom of West Dog Canyon, you'll see the junction with the Marcus Trail. Take a left (south) and head for the heart of the Guadalupe Mountains. Be careful you take the Marcus Trail and not the Bush Mountain Trail, which continues on in a southerly direction. The Marcus Trail is a reclaimed jeep road, which means the grade is not that steep, but it's steadily uphill all the way to the Blue Ridge Trail.

The Marcus Trail is actually an abandoned jeep road.

Upper end of West Dog Canyon from the Marcus Trail.

Parts of the first half of the trail to Blue Ridge can be difficult to find, so be alert for cairns, especially where the trail leaves the valley floor and switchbacks up to the ridge on the west side of West Dog Canyon. After a mile or so on the ridge, the trail enters the high-altitude forest of the Guadalupes and turns into a delightful path carpeted with pine needles and oak leaves. It stays like this until you hit the Blue Ridge Trail.

At the Blue Ridge junction, turn left (east) and head down 0.5 mile to the Tejas Trail junction. Take a left (north) here, and go another 0.7 mile to the Mescalero Camp on your right. Mescalero Camp has eight tent sites with Number 1 offering the best view and most privacy.

After an enjoyable night at the Mescalero Camp, get up early to take advantage of the cool morning air as you head north back to the trailhead. Hiking early and quietly increases your chances of seeing elk, deer, turkey, and other wildlife common in this area. On your right on your way to the junction with McKittrick Canyon Trail are the spectacular upper reaches of South McKittrick Canyon, preserved as a Research Natural Area by the NPS with no entry allowed. This one spot in the Guadalupes will remain totally untrammeled by *Homo sapiens*.

At the junction with the McKittrick Canyon Trail, take a left and continue through the rich forest toward Lost Peak. Shortly beyond Lost Peak, the forest opens up and you switchback down a ridge into the depths of Dog Canyon, coming out at Dog Canyon Springs. From that point on, you follow the easy grade of the canyon bottom all the way to the trailhead.

20 THE TEJAS TRAIL

Type of trail: Shuttle.

Type of trip: Long day hike or overnighter.

| See Map on Page 108 |

Total distance: 11.4 miles.

Difficulty: Difficult day trip or moderate overnighter.

Elevation change: 1,510 feet.

Time required: 7-10 hours.

Maps: Trails Illustrated Guadalupe Mountains Map and USGS Guadalupe Peak and the park brochure.

Starting point: Dog Canyon Trailhead.

Key points:

0.1 Junction with Bush Mountain Trail.

1.5 Dog Canyon Spring.

3.0 Lost Peak.

3.9 Junction with the McKittrick Ridge Trail.

4.7 Mescalero Camp.

5.4 Junction with Blue Ridge Trail.

6.2 Tejas Camp.

6.5 Junction with Juniper Trail.

7.7 Junction with the Bowl and Bush Mountain trails.

11.3 Junction with Frijole Trail.

11.4 Pine Springs Trailhead.

The trail: If you want to walk all the way through the Guadalupe Mountains, this is the shortest route and easiest route with the least possible elevation gain, mainly because the Dog Canyon Trailhead is at a fairly high elevation (6,290 feet).

Regrettably, however, it involves a difficult shuttle. The best way to take this trip would be to make a deal with another party to meet at the Tejas Camp and trade keys so you can drive each other's vehicle to a rendezvous point. If this option isn't available, however, you'll simply have to beg or buy a ride to Dog Canyon, leaving your vehicle at Pine Springs. It will be worth the money or humility. This is a great trip. You can make this a long day hike, but you'll probably enjoy it more as an overnighter.

After getting your backcountry permit from the ranger station at Dog Canyon or the Pine Springs Visitor Center, try to start early. As you quietly walk along the riparian zone of Dog Canyon, you're likely to see wild turkey, mule deer, and other wildlife.

The relict, high-altitude forest of the Guadalupe Mountains.

You leave the gradual grade of the canyon bottom at Dog Canyon Springs, as the trail takes a sharp right turn and starts switchbacking up an open ridge leading to Lost Peak. Just before Lost Peak, the trail enters the forest and stays there until you reach the edge of the escarpment above Pine Springs Canyon. This stretch may be the best trail in the Guadalupes. It's fairly level for 5 miles, well-maintained, and not rocky like some trails in the park.

About a mile past Lost Peak, you hit the junction with the McKittrick Canyon Trail. Turn right and keep going south on the Tejas Trail.

In 0.8 mile, you go by the Mescalero Camp on your left. You can stay here, but the Tejas Camp is more centrally located 1.5 mile down the trail. When you reach the junction with the Blue Ridge Trail, 0.7 mile past the Mescalero Camp, take a left and keep heading south on the Tejas Trail for another 0.8 mile to the Tejas Camp.

The Tejas Camp has four tent sites with number 1 providing the best view. In the camp, you'll find an old water tank, a reminder of early ranching activities in the area.

Shortly after you leave the Tejas Camp, you hit the junction with the Juniper Trail. (Although this trail description covers the Tejas Trail all the way to Pine Springs, there is an alternative route. At this point, you could lengthen your trip by 1 mile and follow the Juniper Trail down Bear Canyon Trail and back to the Pine Springs Trailhead via the Frijole and Foothill trails.) To stay on the Tejas Trail, take a right at this junction, and enjoy your last 1.5 mile of forest-lined trail until you hit the junction with the Bowl Trail at the edge of the escarpment overlooking the Pine Springs area.

At this point, you might want to drop your pack, and take a short side trip to the "best view in Texas" from the top of Hunter Peak. From the junction, it's a 2-mile round trip to Hunter Peak and back—and well worth it. (On the alternative route, the side trip to Hunter Peak is only 1 mile total, which cancels out the extra mileage and makes the two routes almost exactly the same distance.)

After the side trip and a good rest, head down the escarpment on a well-constructed trail, leaving the relict forest of the Guadalupes behind. You trade the quiet serenity of the forest for the awesome vistas of the upper stretches of this trail. You get great views of Pine Springs Canyon, plus Guadalupe, Shumard, and Bartlett peaks, which highlight the ridge on the other side of the canyon. You also get a great chance to study the sharp contrast between the vegetative community of the high plateau and the desert below.

At the bottom of the canyon, you hit the junction with the Frijole Trail. Take a right, staying on the Tejas Trail across the gigantic dry wash of Pine Springs Canyon where you hit another junction. Turn left and you are at Pine Springs Trailhead in another 100 feet.

21 DOG CANYON TO MCKITTRICK CANYON

Type of trail: Shuttle.
Type of trip: Long day hike or overnighter.
Total distance: 14.9 miles.
Difficulty: Difficult day trip or moderate overnighter.
Elevation change: 1,426 feet.
Time required: 8-10 hours.
Maps: Trails Illustrated Guadalupe Mountains Map and USGS Guadalupe Peak and Independence Spring and the park brochure.
Starting point: Dog Canyon Trailhead.

Key points:
- 0.1 Junction with Bush Mountain Trail.
- 3.0 Lost Peak.
- 3.9 Junction with the McKittrick Canyon Trail.
- 7.4 McKittrick Ridge Camp.
- 11.5 The Grotto.
- 12.6 Pratt Lodge.
- 14.9 McKittrick Canyon Trailhead.

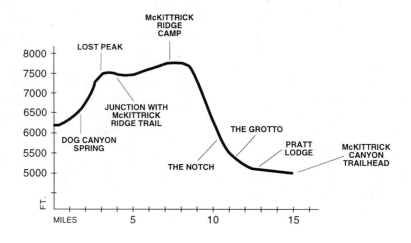

The trail: This is a great way to get the ultimate view of McKittrick Canyon because you don't have to climb up "The Big Sweat," the steep climb out of McKittrick Canyon. However, it involves a problematic shuttle.

The first order of business is to arrange that shuttle. You have to get yourself to Dog Canyon and arrange for a pick-up or a vehicle to be left at McKittrick Canyon Visitor Center. You can also do a "trade keys" trip with friends or relatives and camp together at McKittrick Ridge Camp, but this plan may result in a drawn-out debate over who gets to start at Dog Canyon. The loser has to face the nearly 2,600-foot climb out of McKittrick Canyon. You can get your backcountry camping permit at either Dog Canyon Ranger Station (just north of the trailhead) or the Pine Springs Visitor Center.

Immediately after leaving the Dog Canyon Trailhead on the Tejas Trail, you hit the junction with the Bush Mountain Trail. You take a left and follow narrowing Dog Canyon until the trail turns sharply to the right at Dog Canyon Spring and starts climbing out of the canyon. In another 1.5 miles of steady climbing, you might be ready for a break. If so, drop you pack and hike a short distance to the top of Lost Peak for a good rest and a great view. Then, continue on for another mile to the junction with the McKittrick Canyon Trail.

Turn left (east) here and follow the fairly level trail along McKittrick Ridge. Virtually all the way to McKittrick Ridge Camp, you have good views of the entire Guadalupe high country, especially the upper reaches of South McKittrick Canyon.

You could do this trail in one, long day, but most hikers prefer to stay overnight at McKittrick Ridge Camp, which is on your left 3.5 miles after leaving the Tejas Trail. Even though the camp is nestled in a elegant grove of trees, the view from the camp

Looking down into Dog Canyon from the Tejas Trail.

Dog Canyon to McKittrick Canyon

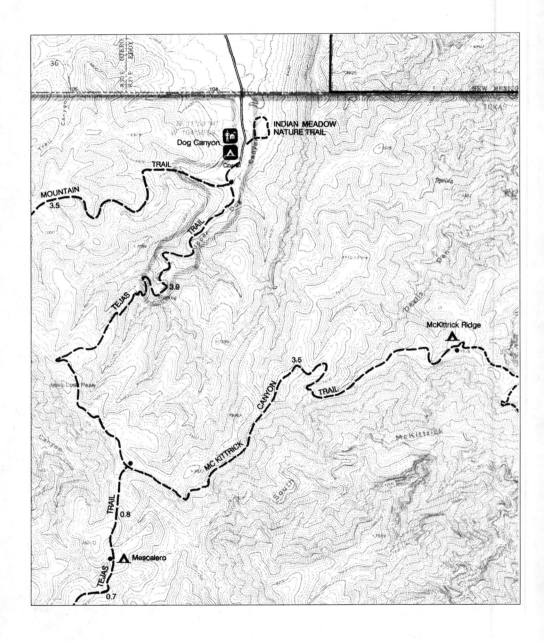

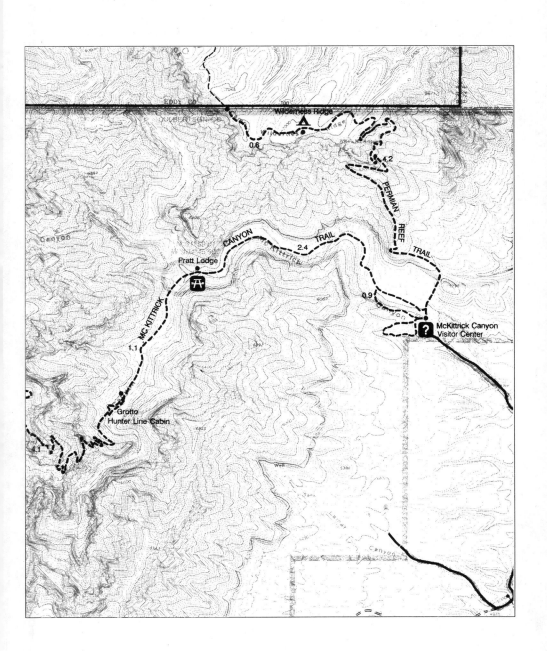

Wilderness Ridge

0.6

4.2

PERMIAN REEF TRAIL

Canyon

Pratt Lodge

McKITTRICK CANYON TRAIL

2.4

0.9

McKittrick Canyon
Visitor Center

MC KITTRICK

1.1

Grotto
Hunter Line Cabin

is inferior to the view from the trail. The camp has eight tent sites with number 1 and number 8 providing the most privacy.

After leaving camp the next morning, you pass through a forest that blocks much of the view for a mile or so. Then, you break out of the trees and before you is the hidden jewel of the Guadalupes, McKittrick Canyon. From up here you can see that the north-facing slopes of the canyon support more riparian species than the drier south-facing slopes.

The view stays with you like a panoramic movie screen for the next 2 miles as you descend the Big Sweat. You will be elated that you didn't do the trip in reverse.

After 4.1 miles, you see a spur trail to the right leading to The Grotto. You'll want to drop your pack here and hike the 0.25 mile to The Grotto (which is like a cave caught above ground) and Hunter Line Cabin. A 5,632-acre gift by the Pratt family and a 70,000-acre purchase from the Hunter family combined to form the bulk of what is now Guadalupe Mountains National Park.

At The Grotto, you find a unique feature of the arid Guadalupes—a live stream flows out of the canyon that's large enough to support a population of rainbow trout. The stream stays on your right for another 1.1 miles, until you reach another short spur trail to your left going to Pratt Lodge. Here, you can take a long breather and picnic on the stone tables found near the lodge. After leaving the stately Pratt Lodge, it's an easy 2.3 miles to the McKittrick Canyon visitor Center. Over these last miles, the stream magically disappears and reappears several times.

Make sure you plan your trip to leave enough time to drive the 4.5 miles from the visitor center to U.S. Highway 62\180. The NPS locks the gate at 6 p.m. MDT or 4:30 p.m. MST.

AFTERWORD

A BAD IDEA?

It has been whispered here and there, usually by "locals," that books like this are a bad idea.

The theory goes something like this: Guidebooks bring more people into the wilderness; more people cause more environmental damage; and the wildness we all seek gradually evaporates.

I used to think like that, too. Here's why I changed my mind.

When I wrote and published my first guidebook in 1979 (*The Hiker's Guide to Montana*), some of my hiking buddies disapproved. Since then, I've published more than 40 hiking guides, and I'm proud of it.

I also hope these books have increased wilderness use.

Many experienced hikers tend to have a lofty attitude toward the inexperienced masses. They think anybody who wants to backpack can buy a topo map and compass and find their own way through the wilderness. But the fact is, most people want a guide. Sometimes, inexperienced hikers prefer a real, live person to show them the way and help them build confidence, but most of the time, they can get by with a trail guide like this one.

All guidebooks published by Falcon (and most published by other publishers) invite wilderness users to respect and support the protection of wild country. Sometimes, this is direct editorializing. Sometimes, this invitation takes the more subtle form of simply helping people experience wilderness. And it's a rare person who leaves the wilderness without a firmly planted passion for wild country—and a desire to vote for more of it.

In classes on backpacking taught for the Yellowstone Institute, I have taken hundreds of people into the wilderness. Often, they were wearing a backpack for the first time, and many of them were not convinced of the need for more wilderness, but they were all convinced when we arrived back at the trailhead.

Many, many times, I've seen it happen without saying a single word about wilderness. It doesn't take preaching. We just need to get people out into the wilderness where the essence of wildness sort of sneaks up on your heart and takes root, and before you know it, it's too late. You're converted.

But what about overcrowding? Yes, it's a problem in many places and probably will be in Carlsbad Caverns and Guadalupe Mountains. The answer to overcrowded, overused wilderness is not restrictive regulations limiting use of wilderness. The answer is more wilderness.

How can we convince people to support more wilderness when they have never experienced wilderness. In my opinion, we can't. Without the support of people who experience wilderness, there will be no more wilderness.

That's why we need guidebooks. And that's why I changed by mind. I now believe guidebooks have done as much to build support for wilderness as pro-wilderness organizations have ever done through political and public relation efforts.

And if that's not enough, here's another reason. All FalconGuides (and most guidebooks from other publishers) contain sections on no trace camping and wilderness safety. Guidebooks provide an ideal medium for communicating this vital information to the inexperienced.

In 30 years of backpacking, I have seen dramatic changes in how backpackers care for wilderness. I've seen it go from appalling to exceptional. Today, almost everybody walks softly in the wilderness. And I believe the information contained in guidebooks has been partly responsible for this change.

Having said all that, I hope many thousands of people use this book to enjoy a fun-filled vacation hiking Carlsbad Caverns or Guadalupe Mountains national parks—and then, of course, vote for wilderness preservation the rest of their lives.

—Bill Schneider, Publisher
Falcon Press

ABOUT THE AUTHOR

LIVING LIFE ONE MILE AT A TIME

The author on top of Guadalupe Peak.

Whenever Bill Schneider isn't out in the wilderness, he wants to be. He has spent over 30 years hiking trails all across America.

In his college days in the late 1960s, he worked on a trail crew in Glacier National Park. He spent the 1970s publishing the *Montana Outdoors Magazine* for the Montana Department of Fish, Wildlife & Parks and covering as many miles of trails as possible on weekends and holidays.

In 1979, Bill and his partner Mike Sample established Falcon Press Publishing and published two guidebooks the first year. Bill wrote one of them, *The Hiker's Guide to Montana*—which is still a popular guidebook. He has also written six more books and many magazine articles on wildlife, outdoor recreation, and environmental issues. Along the way, on a part-time basis over a span of 12 years, Bill has taught classes on bicycling, backpacking, no trace camping, and hiking in bear country for The Yellowstone Institute, a nonprofit educational organization in Yellowstone National Park.

Since 1979, Bill has served as publisher of Falcon Press, which is now established as a premier publisher of recreational guidebooks with nearly 300 titles in print.

BRING ALONG A COMPANION

On your next trip to the great outdoors, bring along *Wild Country Companion*. This new FalconGuide includes state-of-the-art methods for safe, no-trace traveling in North America's backcountry. Whether you're on foot, horse or bike, this book offers new ways to sustain our outdoor recreation resources.

Wild Country Companion
By Will Harmon
Illustrated by
Lisa Harvey
160 pp., 6 x 9",
charts, softcover.

For more information on this and other Falcon Press books visit your local bookstore. Or call 1-800-582-2665

TRAILS ILLUSTRATED
TOPO MAPS

Unlock the wilderness. Whether you're pursuing off-trail adventure in the Chihuahuan Desert or just out for a casual hike along Old Guano Road Trail, these maps are the key to exciting wilderness adventure in Guadalupe Moutains & Carlsbad Caverns National Parks.

accurate • wear and tear proof waterproof • up-to-date
$8.99

To order, contact your local outdoor retailer or call Falcon at
1-800-582-2665.

FALCON P.O. Box 1718, Helena, MT 59624